THE
sweet
spot

Leveraging Your Talents in Leadership and Life

Whitney Walpole
and Laureli Shimayo

with Shannon Harrison

RED DOT PRESS

For information, please contact:

Red Dot Press
www.RedDotPress.biz
www.culturecounts.biz
www.ThriveTypes.com

600 South Cherry Street, Suite 305
Glendale, CO 80246
303-872-7926

Library of Congress Control Number: 2016936465

Walpole, Whitney, Shimayo, Laureli, and Harrison, Shannon
The Sweet Spot: Leveraging Your Talents in Leadership and Life / by Whitney Walpole and
Laureli Shimayo with Shannon Harrison. p. cm.

ISBN 978-0-9968261-7-4

CONTENTS

A NOTE FROM THE AUTHORS

In many ways, our subject is not a new one. What we refer to as a person's "Talents" are based on existing archetype categories that have been written and spoken about for centuries.

So why say more?

In our search to support the many people who have wanted a deeper dive into our Sweet Spot work, we discovered that the existing books on related subjects weren't focused on leadership and didn't reflect the depth of distinction that we use in our work.

The time is ripe for a modern update to this ancient subject, and we realized we were just the people to do it. After working with thousands of leaders, clients and entrepreneurs, from large organizations to start-ups, we have taken what is known about each of the Talents to a whole new level.

With Laureli's acumen for acquiring and systematizing knowledge and her laser-sharp eye for observing subtleties, combined with Whitney's gift for making things simple, practical and accessible, we've described the richness of each Talent in ways that go beyond what's provided in the books we have encountered to date. We also found a need to explain the complexities of the Talents in ways that are easy to understand and connect with and that can be applied personally and professionally—particularly as they pertain to leadership. Moreover, it was important to us to present a map of the Talents that is simple, but not simplistic, and allows for the wide range of diversity and uniqueness found in people.

What makes the work in this book powerful and worth sharing is that we have had the fortune of having decades of experience with leaders, individuals and organizations in putting this rich awareness into action—applying this knowledge daily, on the field, consistently and with tangible success.

Today our business grows substantially every year—something neither of us could have done alone. More importantly, it's something neither of us could have done together without the knowledge of our different Sweet Spots and our Talents. First and foremost, we use this work on ourselves. We are constantly delighted by the way we are able to collaborate together and leverage our differences. Whitney is masterful at helping others articulate their vision and inspiring them to build that vision, and Laureli leveraged these gifts to take her own work out into the world with greater power and impact than she had ever experienced. Laureli is a genius at mapping information into patterns for building replicable systems, and Whitney harnessed these gifts to expand her own work far beyond what she knew was possible. In much the same way that steel braided together becomes exponentially stronger than individual strands, we have woven our Talents together in a partnership that capitalizes on the best of what each has to offer.

But this was not always the case. Laureli originally cringed when people like Whitney started in with the "vision" and "potential" talk. Whitney used to run the other way when people like Laureli started in with details and data. And yet today there is a deep appreciation between both of us for what we each provide. This appreciation has led to a partnership with an unprecedented level of productivity, joy and financial reward that exceeded what either one of us imagined possible. We are now thriving because of our differences, not despite them.

This book reflects some of the best work we have done together, the ideas that have made the most direct and profound difference in people's lives and businesses, and one of the conversations we most want to share with the world.

Whatever you may do with the information in this book, be it create a core shift in how you relate to yourself, a significant leap in your business's growth or a fundamental change at a global level—we walk with you, as partners, on the journey to building a world where people are recognized and honored for their unique contributions.

Whitney & Laureli

INTRODUCTION

THE SWEET SPOT

It's all about the Sweet Spot.

You probably already have a sense of what the Sweet Spot is. The minute you hear the phrase, it may conjure up images of times in the past when you were "on top of your game" or when "things came together easily."

Every golfer knows an aspect of the Sweet Spot—where the "sweet spot" is on the face of the club that has the ball sail into the green. Every tennis player knows the "sweet spot" on the face of the racket that sends a killer serve. Musicians call it being "in the pocket"—when the rhythm is right and the musicians are locked into one another. Writers call it "being in the flow." In this space, there is no sense of time passing, no sense of stress or distress. It is total focus without strain.

But this is only one aspect of the Sweet Spot.

The Sweet Spot we're talking about in this book has similarities, but it is different from "the zone" or "the pocket." What the golfer senses and what the musician senses is only a part of a larger theme. What we are pointing to is something that is a much more central part of your being than a particular skill you have or something you do. It is something that is always true about you, no matter what situation you're in. We're talking about a fundamental core of who you are.

When you are finally able to see your Sweet Spot, you'll realize that it pervades every area of your life. It's a doorway to your most natural gifts. Your deep well of extraordinary strength and capacity. Your greatest contributions. Your quickest access to joy and fulfillment.

And here's the good news—everyone has a Sweet Spot.

And even better news—it's easy to see.

This book is designed to do just this—to help you see yourself clearly, bring your most powerful qualities to the forefront of your awareness, and enable you to leverage them in the world. And living and working from your Sweet Spot isn't selfish. It not only benefits you; it benefits everyone.

One client described the Sweet Spot this way: "Realizing my Sweet Spot was like realizing I had lungs that served the purpose of breathing, nerves that served the purpose of sending signals. My Sweet Spot didn't occur like some elusive spiritual element but like an inherent part of who I am, like I was wired this way from the get-go. This has had countless repercussions, one of the most useful being my ability to relax into who I am rather than fighting myself."

Keep in mind that first and foremost, the purpose of this book is to identify *your* Sweet Spot. Inevitably, you will also begin to recognize the Sweet Spots of those around you. When you see the Sweet Spot in others, you will experience profound appreciation for who they are and what they have to offer.

Despite all its uses, the Sweet Spot is not a system for pigeonholing you or other people into personality types. It will, however, help you understand who is likely to be better at certain things, who enjoys them more and who is more likely to be sustainably successful at each activity and, ultimately, more fulfilled.

For those in leadership positions, this book provides powerful insights into how others operate and what makes them tick. While it shouldn't be the only word on whom to hire and fire, it can help you see who is likely to be a better fit for a particular position, team and culture. Additionally, it can help you solve HR challenges and discover how to support people to work together more easily and productively. Knowing your people's Sweet Spots will help you better manage, coach and motivate them every day.

THE 7 TALENTS OF THE SWEET SPOT

A person's Sweet Spot is the sum total of many characteristics. The most important characteristic for determining someone's Sweet Spot is what we call their natural Talents. Talents are based on archetypes—universal symbols that represent specific patterns of values and behaviors. These Talent archetypes offer a rich map of who people are and how they can grow.

There are a total of 7 Talents, and each of them makes an equally valuable and distinct contribution. Every person has 3 of these Talents, and they are the most essential building blocks of their Sweet Spot.

The names we use for the 7 Talents are common terms that we find people easily remember.

The goal is to find which 3 Talents are most true for you and begin to mine these gifts for their richness, to savor and express their inherent power.

Keep in mind that you'll likely reveal your Sweet Spot in layers.

It's not about getting it exactly right. It's a journey of exploring who you are and uncovering what's true for you.

Having a full awareness of your Sweet Spot won't just provide a one-time insight but can also be used to map your journey of personal and professional growth for years.

If you would like additional support at any point on your journey, you are welcome to contact us (see page 219).

HOW TO READ THIS BOOK

This book is not meant to be read from cover to cover without pause. You may read one or two paragraphs, set the book down, let yourself digest and integrate, and then come back to read again. You may also want to keep this book by your desk as a reference tool for situations that arise in the future.

As you read about each of the 7 Talents, you may find that you identify at some level with all of them. See if you can narrow down what resonates more for you and what resonates less.

While you are reading, notice how much you experience:

- "Yes, that's me!" (exhilaration)
- "I wish I were or should be more like that." (envy)
- "No, that's not me." (neutrality or repulsion)

If you notice you feel exhilarated, you might consider this Talent as part of your Sweet Spot. If you notice reactions of envy or repulsion, consider these Talents might not be yours.

Another way to find what resonates for you is to try to put aside what you've been told all your life. Put aside what you believe you should do, are highly trained in or are good at. While you read each chapter, try on each Talent and imagine behaving as if it's part of you.

While you imagine trying on a Talent, notice how you feel:

- Energized or drained?
- Alive or dull?
- At ease or tense?

If you feel energized, alive and at ease, consider this Talent for your Sweet Spot. If you feel drained, dull or tense, you might wonder about this Talent. It may not be yours.

Consider making notes in the chapters as you read, or use the chart found in Synthesizing Your Reflections on page 204.

Keep in mind—this is just the beginning. The basic information on the 7 Talents is here. If you want to explore further, we do Sweet Spot Assessments as well as individual and team coaching. For now, know that the information in this book alone can lead to profound and impactful shifts for you, your people and your organization.

TAKING OFF THE MASK

Most of us are already aware that as human beings we put on "masks"—ways that we have learned to respond and behave that aren't part of our natural self-expression. This is true with Talents as well. A person can try to express a particular Talent, and even develop some skill with it; however, they won't feel as energized or at ease as someone who naturally has it.

An important step to finding your Sweet Spot is to identify your Masks.

Masks typically

- come **from childhood**—usually from our family of origin and our culture
- are ways we adapted **to get the love and attention** we needed while growing up (for example, almost everyone in the United States has some Scholar Masking from our educational system)
- are ways that have **felt comfortable and safe**—maybe we even experienced **some success** with these ways, but often at a personal and sometimes physical **cost**
- occur as what we *should* be or *should* do and often create a sense of **anxiety** when we are not or do not
- lead us to choose careers, companies, employees, romantic relationships and even leisure activities that require **hard work** and leave us dissatisfied
- are **no match** for someone who operates from this Talent naturally—even if we can keep pace for a while, we'll be the

one who runs out of steam

- are **annoying to others** because they can sense we are incongruent, that something is off

You are likely operating from a Mask if you

- feel drained, tired and stressed
- have physical pain or tension (e.g., headaches)
- lose credibility with people
- create unnecessary conflict
- spend a lot of effort for little result
- sense time is moving at a snail's pace
- feel trapped

If you don't recognize your Masks now, you'll likely discover them as you read about all the Talents. Masks become much more obvious and less interesting when you get a taste of the joy and fulfillment of operating from your true Talents.

THE 7 TALENTS IN THE WORKPLACE: THE STORY OF GLOBALAPP

To best illustrate the Talents as they would apply in a typical business situation, we created the story of GlobalApp.

The company GlobalApp and its employees, leaders and clients are purely fictional; however, they are based on real scenarios that we have observed in the nearly two decades of working with thousands of businesses. Each GlobalApp team member has a different Talent, and each chapter begins with a story told from that team member's perspective.

GlobalApp's story is a common one. As a successful tech company and a pioneer in the industry, the company has been experiencing rapid acceleration and, as a result, the growing pains that come along with it. Most of these breakdowns have been minor—until now. Recently, one of their largest clients terminated their service contract.

Brian, the CEO and mastermind behind GlobalApp's innovative products, personally recruited and hired each of the six executives on his leadership team. In the face of losing a key client, however, what has come to light is how different all of these leaders actually are—what they value, how they view what the underlying problems are, what they believe the company needs to do to move forward and how they express their opinions.

Despite the fact that GlobalApp continues to grow, it is becoming apparent that the current crisis may be a reflection of what is going on with the leadership team. Although the team is filled with ex-

traordinarily accomplished, competent people, they are seven different leaders operating in their own silos, and this is causing the work culture to slowly erode while clients are falling through the cracks.

Under pressure from several of his leaders, Brian decides that the best thing to do is get everyone on the team together for an off-site retreat. As the meeting takes place, it becomes obvious that each leader is operating from a different set of perspectives. With little understanding of each other's Talents, the company meeting begins to erode in predictable ways; this leaves the team feeling frustrated and their contributions unrecognized and underutilized.

GlobalApp, like many companies, would benefit enormously from gaining in-depth knowledge of the Talents on the team—how to identify them, appreciate them and leverage their rich contributions.

CHAPTER 1

THE ARTISAN

BRIAN, CEO OF GLOBALAPP

Day of GlobalApp's corporate retreat:

All of my senior leaders are looking at me, waiting for me to get this meeting started. I know we need to be here, but, truth be told, I would rather be back with the product development team working on something new. At the same time, I would do anything for this company. This is my baby. These are the people who have brought my ideas to life, and we have been really successful.

The recent loss of one of our key clients, someone who signed with us during the early stages of the company, has hit me hard and indicates a big problem that needs to be solved. In that sense, I am anxious to hear what new ideas the team generates.

At breakfast this morning, Dave and I started talking about a new function we could incorporate into our existing product. "I love this idea!" I told him. "I wonder if I can bring it up while everyone's in the same room and throw it out there for feedback. Maybe I'll try to get it in there at the end." However, I know I've got to stay focused on the agenda, at least for a little while, or I'm going to tick the others off. I've done it before.

"Okay, everyone," I say to open up the meeting, "let's jump right in. You know we lost a key client recently, and that means that we, as a company, fell short somewhere. I want to hear ideas from each of you about what you think GlobalApp's biggest problem is that needs to be solved so that this doesn't happen again."

After a while, everyone on the team has given me their take on our biggest problem, and we now have what I was after: a good-sized pool of ideas. Some of them I found interesting, and others I didn't even want to listen to. As long as the solution doesn't stifle our creativity or innovation, I'm open. To me, having spent the time getting a lot of ideas on the table is time well spent; however, there are others on the team that are visibly annoyed. Maria, the Director of Operations, comments, "Brian, I don't see the point of this. We haven't narrowed down these ideas or assigned actions to any of them."

Ugh. I can see Maria's point. A few minutes ago, I was feeling pretty good about this meeting; now all I feel is angst.

What contribution is Brian making, and what unique value does he bring?

What is Brian overly focused on or attached to that is causing frustration?

THE ARTISAN'S CONTRIBUTIONS

> Those who dream by day are
> cognizant of many things that escape
> those who dream only at night.
> *Edgar Allan Poe*

Artisans are often described as "living in a world of their own," yet they make significant contributions to the world around them. They can make great inventors, innovators and artists in whatever field they choose and are not limited by any means to what we might traditionally think of as "artisan" or "artist" professions, such as painting or sculpting. Their mode of thinking is not often restricted by convention, so they are able to see solutions that others miss. Artisans tend to promote beauty and harmony, inviting others into the freedom of expression they seek for themselves. Because they are so comfortable with change and the fluidity of life, well-developed Artisans can be excellent facilitators of change whether it is within a family, a corporation or a culture.

> To raise new questions, new possibilities,
> to regard old problems from a new angle,
> requires creative imagination and marks real
> advance in science.
> *Albert Einstein*

Because an Artisan's way of processing the world can be so unique, their ideas and solutions are typically **innovative and exciting**. They can bring a vibrant energy to all they do in contrast to the lackluster, conventional ideas and creations of their peers. Malcolm Gladwell, author of *Blink* and *The Tipping Point*, among other best sellers, began as a journalist, and his first assignment was to write a piece about fashion. Instead of following the norm and writing about high-end fashion and well-known designers, Gladwell chose to write an innovative piece about a man who manufactured T-shirts. In his perspective, "It was much more interesting to write a piece about someone who made a T-shirt for $8 than it was to write about a dress that costs $100,000. I mean, you or I could make a dress for $100,000, but to make a T-shirt for $8—that's much tougher."

> Innovation distinguishes between
> a leader and a follower.
> *Steve Jobs*

Steve Jobs's innovations created excitement in the market for decades and left many people anxiously anticipating what he would come up with next and lining up to purchase Apple's products. He captured the imagination of customers by offering them something they didn't even know they needed. The iPad was developed as a new kind of technology to allow airline pilots, mechanics and physicians to carry a single, small device rather than having to lug around heavy manuals or charts. Jobs then mentally modeled a new market—media consumption. He positioned the iPad not to replace the laptop or phone but to fill a "need" that caused a buzz, while creating a brand-new market segment.

Another Artisan, Buckminster Fuller, was a 20th century architect, systems theorist, author, designer, inventor and futurist who presented hundreds of innovative and exciting alternatives to existing designs. His breakthrough Dymaxion map showed the earth's continents with minimum distortion when projected or printed on a flat surface. Fuller's Dymaxion car prototypes were built in 1932. They had two front-drive wheels, one rear wheel and an aerodynamic, tear-shaped body that was large enough to seat eleven people. The cars averaged 30 miles per gallon and reached speeds of 100 miles per hour—unheard of in that era. Of his work, Fuller wrote, "People should think things out fresh and not just accept conventional terms and the conventional way of doing things."

> It's really clear to me that you can't hang on to something longer than its time. Ideas lose certain freshness, ideas have a shelf life, and sometimes they have to be replaced by other ideas.
>
> *Alan Alda*

Artisans' freedom from conventional modes of thinking often allows them to see **options and choices** that others miss. They aren't generally stuck choosing from a menu of traditional options but perceive new possibilities in whatever field they're in. Controversial American financier Michael Milken brought this sensibility to the world of corporate finance, saying, "Financing is an art form. One of the challenges is how to correctly finance a company…sometimes a company should issue convertible bonds instead of straight bonds. Sometimes it should issue preferred stock. Each company and each financing is different, and the process can't be imitative." Milken saw profitable options and choices for financing that others missed. When Milken was charged with securities fraud, his attorney, Harvey A. Silverglate, disputed the allegations, claiming, "Milken's biggest problem was that some of his most ingenious but entirely lawful maneuvers were viewed, by those who initially did not understand them, as felonious, precisely because they were novel—and often extremely profitable."

> I just invent, then wait until man comes
> around to needing what I've invented.
> *R. Buckminster Fuller*

Artisans are typically drawn to **beauty**, and they bring an **aesthetic sensibility** to all they do. In his work on Apple products, Steve Jobs was ultrasensitive about how the look and feel of the products could enhance user experience, from packaging to keystroke pressure to font styles and screen colors. His design aesthetic was influenced by the modernist architect Joseph Eichler, the Buddhism he experienced in India, and the calligraphy classes he took in college, among other things. Jobs's attention to beauty and elegance in design set a new bar for the formerly function-focused tech industry and proved that there was an enormous market for an Artisan's aesthetic in hardware and software. Today, Apple boasts that "the back of our computer looks better than the front of anyone else's."

When I am working on a problem, I never think about beauty but when I have finished, if the solution is not beautiful, I know it is wrong.

R. Buckminster Fuller

Biographers say that Einstein was driven to most of his scientific conclusions by the conviction that nature displayed a beauty that was discernible and that a characteristic feature of this beauty was simplicity. One of his contemporaries, physicist Max Planck, wrote that in Einstein's general theory of relativity "the intimate union between the beautiful, the true and the real has again been proved."

DOS is ugly and interferes with users' experience.

Bill Gates

Artisans can be extremely **entrepreneurial**, often juggling many balls at once. Buckminster Fuller not only designed a variety of cutting-edge products, but he published 30 books, taught at several universities, lectured internationally and manufactured his geodesic domes for everything from Arctic weather stations to playgrounds.

Since the demise of the Beatles, Paul McCartney released an extensive catalog as a solo artist, composed classical and electronic music, and has taken part in numerous projects to promote international charities related to animal rights, seal hunting, landmines, vegetarianism, poverty and music education.

The über-entrepreneurial Steve Jobs knew enough about electronics to be involved in hardware and enough about programming to be involved in software. He was involved as well in marketing and branding and personally oversaw much of Apple's marketing efforts from the nuts and bolts of billboards and magazine spreads to TV commercials. Then, of course, he was also notoriously involved in aesthetics and design. In addition to all of the other hats Jobs wore, he still managed to devote a huge amount of his time and energy to imbue all features of Apple products with extraordinary style and elegance. Being able to fluidly provide leadership and talent in so many areas of a company is one of the qualities of an Artisan that enabled Jobs to excel as an entrepreneur.

> I do not like to repeat successes,
> I like to go on to other things.
> *Walt Disney*

Freedom on many levels can be vitally important to Artisans. They tend to flourish when their creativity is unbound and untethered. Isadora Duncan spoke for all Artisans when she said, "My motto—sans limites!" Freedom for an Artisan usually includes a sense of movement and fluidity, the capacity for change and an ever-evolving flow of form and ideas that brings them life. Within this freedom, Artisans can be passionate about **self-expression**. For the most part, they have no desire to fit into preconceived molds but love to break molds so they can define themselves as the unique individuals they are. Many of the greats we consider "artists" in the traditional sense, from Bob Dylan to Michael Jackson, have connected with the masses through their creative freedom and self-expression. Great Artisans such as Einstein and Stephen Hawking brought this same passion for creative freedom and self-expression to manifest extraordinary breakthroughs in science.

> The creative is the place where no one
> else has ever been. You have to leave the
> city of your comfort and go into the
> wilderness of your intuition.
> *Alan Alda*

THE ARTISAN UNDERBELLY

As brilliant and creative as Artisans can be, they can also have traits that make them difficult to deal with. Before they have found their niche where they can fully express their ingenuity, Artisans are often **rebellious and uncooperative**. As a teenager, Einstein clashed with school authorities. He forged a note from a doctor so the school would let him leave and join his family in Italy. In grade school, Steve Jobs was deemed an "insubordinate" student who spent more time playing pranks on others than doing his homework.

Beyond being uncooperative, an Artisan's rebellion may take them into **risky experimentation**, possibly with drugs, sex or choices of friends. Urban legend has it that Jimi Hendrix put hits of LSD inside his headband so that they would seep into his pores during concerts and that he occasionally cut his head above his brow to give the hits a direct line to his mind.

Artisans can have an intense **desire to stand out** and be different, rebelling against being boxed in or labeled in any way. Internally, they can convince themselves that they are unusual and separate from everyone else, but this also leads them to feel **lonely** and like no one understands them.

> I never felt comfortable with myself, because I was never part of the majority. I always felt awkward and shy and on the outside of the momentum of my friends' lives.
> *Steven Spielberg*

Artisans are often seen as **procrastinators**, leaving projects until big bursts of activity happen at the last minute. Rather than working steadily in ways that others understand, they often percolate, waiting for the muse to hit, and then dash to the finish line. At Harvard, Bill Gates was reported to have no study regimen. Instead, he got by on a few hours of sleep, crammed for his tests and passed with reasonable grades. Students who knew Stephen

Hawking in college reported that he often read science fiction when he was supposed to be working on complex school assignments—yet he could always complete the assignments just in time for class.

> I've had periods in my life when I've had a bundle of ideas come along, and I've had long dry spells. If I get an idea next week, I'll do something. If not, I won't do a damn thing.
>
> *Warren Buffett*

Artisans can be **moody and overly sensitive**. Their internal emotional lives are often intense, and they can be easily upset or overwhelmed by their environments. Bill Gates's parents worried that he was becoming depressed and withdrawn in grade school. Stephen Hawking was similarly reclusive and unhappy in his first year in college. At age 27, Buckminster Fuller seriously considered suicide so that his family could receive the money from his life insurance.

Vincent Van Gogh's brother described the artist's erratic moods in a letter: "It seems as if he were two persons: one, marvelously gifted, tender and refined, the other, egotistic and hard-hearted. They present themselves in turns, so that one hears him talk first in one way, then in the other, and always with arguments on both sides."

Artisans have a strong tendency to get **bored** easily and can become restless and disinterested if they are not challenged or focused on their unique interests. At 17, Stephen Hawking found his academic work at Oxford "ridiculously easy." His physics tutor, Robert Berman, said, "It was only necessary for him to know that something could be done, and he could do it without looking to see how other people did it."

> Once a month the sky falls on my head, I come to and I see another movie I want to make.
> *Steven Spielberg*

Artisans often reject boredom in their personal lives as well. Of her first divorce, actress Marilyn Monroe said, "My marriage didn't make me sad, but it didn't make me happy either. My husband and I hardly spoke to each other. This wasn't because we were angry. We had nothing to say. I was dying of boredom."

Artisans are also accused of being **flighty** and **ungrounded**. Musician Jimi Hendrix was known for being irresponsible and unreliable. Once when he was late for a concert, his manager found him sleeping. "I dreamed the gig was cancelled so I went back to bed," Jimi said. They can be perceived as being easily distracted and following the next bright shiny thing that comes along.

OTHER ARTISAN CHARACTERISTICS

Artisans are typically all about **creativity**. They usually live for the new, the novel and the unique. Artisans are often the first to spot—or begin—a new trend, movement or fashion. They are known to thrive working with original ideas and in environments that are fresh, original and innovative. Whenever we talk about out-of-the-box thinking, Artisans wonder, "What box?" As a result, they usually loathe being micromanaged and resent being "typed" or defined by those outside of themselves.

Artisans are likely to be drawn to **sensual experiences**. They can be intensely aware of all the subtleties of every experience—taste, feel, smell, look and sound—and they delight in the stimulation of exquisite **sensual pleasures** whether it be music, food or sex.

Artisans love adventures. They are not luxuries to Artisans but necessary to life.

***

> The harmony of music exists equally
> with the harmony of movement in nature.
> Man has not invented the harmony of music.
> It is one of the underlying principles of life.
> *Isadora Duncan*

***

Because they are so creative and **spontaneous**, Artisans can appear to have a loose relationship with the truth. They'll often share stories and information differently in each conversation, so others may judge them as being misleading and disingenuous. In actuality, they may have simply changed their minds or just want to keep things interesting.

Artisans tend to be present with what is happening in the moment. This can show up as a fluidity and flow with or zesty passion for what's happening in the moment, as if that is all there is. "What's so" about reality changes rapidly, which can have the effect of making the Artisan seem "flighty" to others.

ARTISAN STAGES OF DEVELOPMENT

STAGE 1: Artisans in this stage seem to be against everything and for nothing. They tend to rebel against anything that smacks of ordinary, traditional or limited in any form, from the clothes they wear to their topics of conversation. Craving a sense of freedom, they often refuse to get involved or commit to any idea or project, which leaves them ineffective and nonproductive. At this stage, they may even rebel against their own ideas.

They can constantly distract themselves with whatever appears to be new or novel. But because they are not yet grounded in their feelings and sensing, they often deceive themselves about what is the next hot thing, flitting from idea to idea rapidly without really landing anywhere. This lack of grounding also means that Artisans can have very short attention spans—except when ferociously defending themselves from being confined in any way. Because they only know what they don't want and not what they do want, Artisans may feel helpless, not empowered and have a difficult time making choices or decisions.

It might be difficult to communicate with Artisans at this stage, but they can be engaged by showing appreciation for their unique perspective and encouraging them to discover what they want. Artisans grow when they are drawn out and helped to see how their ideas might benefit others.

STAGE 2: Artisans in this stage have usually gained strength and have become more adamant about proving their uniqueness and forcing their perspectives on others. Rather than objecting to everything, they now direct their rebellion toward specific people or ideas. Artisans at this stage can get bored easily, which they may express frequently. Most likely, they will still avoid making choices, committing to projects or collaborating with others, preferring to "keep their options open" and their sense of freedom unencumbered.

Stage 2 Artisans can be moody, feeling a sense of torment internally that they often can't articulate. They might be dramatic in their emotions and may instigate drama around them. On the flip side, they may often escape into daydreaming, trying on different personas like chameleons. These Artisans tend to be somewhat selfish and self-centered, and they focus any creative efforts solely on their own needs and desires. They may crave sensual experiences and immerse themselves fully with little or no thought to consequences.

Artisans at this stage benefit by learning to define more clearly and by learning to become more focused on what they want rather than what is wrong with the world. They are also ready to explore how they might find the freedom they require while still being connected to other people and organizations. Stage 2 Artisans are ready to be coached to see the ways in which more of their ideas can manifest and to feel the satisfaction of bringing these ideas into concrete form.

STAGE 3: Artisans in this stage are beginning to offer their unique gifts in ways that are beneficial and productive. Rather than avoiding decisions, they now reinforce their sense of freedom by offering a variety of options and choices. They use their creativity to contribute in ways that are relevant and meaningful to others.

Because these Artisans are so comfortable with fluidity and the shifting sands of life, they are excellent at facilitating change for others. They are also comfortable in the midst of what others see as paradox and can help those around them bridge seemingly unresolvable conflict. Artisans at this stage are quite sensitive, not only to their own internal feelings and urgings, but also to the likely experiences of others. This quality makes them adept at solving problems and being creative for others and also makes them incredibly attractive to the people around them.

Artisans in Stage 3 can be encouraged to honor their inner leanings and preferences more and to pay attention to their own sense of the world—that innate "yes, this is good" or "no, this is not good" that they experience. These Artisans are also ready to learn to prioritize the ideas that they really want to manifest and to apply their gifts (i.e., finding creative solutions around any obstacles that appear) to the projects they undertake. They are also ready to learn to take smaller steps toward their goals and dreams rather than huge, undisciplined, and often imaginary leaps forward.

STAGE 4: Artisans in this stage maintain their creative, spacious presence, yet are much more grounded. They have learned to listen to their internal guidance system and honor their sense of yes and no, so they rarely feel trapped when making a choice. They are clear about what they really want and feel fully capable of bringing their own ideas into form. Not only are they able to appreciate and value the sublime, they are able to easily create it.

Artisans in Stage 4 experience true freedom through the powerful choices they make. They are finally comfortable making what look like commitments to everyone else, because they know they are always free.

ARTISAN SWEET SPOT—KEY POINTS

CORE VALUES & BEHAVIORS
- creativity, ideas, innovation, imagination
- freedom, choice, options
- problem solving, elegant solutions
- pleasure, sensual awareness (taste, feel, smell, look, sound)
- change, spontaneity, bursts of activity
- beauty, aesthetic sensibility

TRIGGERS
- ordinariness, lack of originality
- ugliness, bad design
- being boxed in or limited, repetition
- control, being told what to do, being micromanaged

CHALLENGES
- rebellion, independence erring on lack of cooperation
- taking risks that are too big (or seem too big to others)
- procrastination

- moodiness, oversensitivity, boredom
- distraction, flightiness, fantasy
- making choices and commitments, following through

GREAT ORGANIZATIONAL ROLES

- entrepreneurs—juggling many balls at once, wearing many hats, seeing unique opportunities
- inventors—in all areas they touch, product/service creation
- designers—products, marketing, graphics, environments
- brainstorming, creative problem solving

THE ARTISAN LEADER

- does new things in new ways
- plays many roles
- changes their plans
- is rarely stopped by obstacles
- is motivated when they are told "it can't be done"
- takes risks that others won't
- is willing to hold out for a better outcome, despite chaos and uncertainty

TIPS & COACHING:
LEVERAGING YOUR ARTISAN TALENT

If you discover you've got the Artisan Sweet Spot while reading this chapter, these are ways you can experience the most joy, ease and collaboration and create the best results:

> Give yourself enough **freedom**—Artisans need enough

spontaneous and varied flow to be maximally creative and productive

- Artisan leaders often believe they need to get focused and organized; however, the gift of an Artisan typically shines when things look a bit messy—Artisans are about inventing in fresh open space, and this often doesn't occur on a schedule or in a clean and neat way—don't pressure yourself to fit in the typical leadership mold with everyone else

- Include time and space in your schedule for unstructured thinking, brainstorming, creative exploration, daydreaming and imagining

- Don't pack your schedule with back-to-back meetings or activities—this may seem to you or others like downtime or that you are being unproductive; however, for an Artisan, this is time where the new ideas appear and you nourish your creativity

- Have an area in your life in which you can **be creative and tinker** with no pressure to reach a predetermined outcome so you allow ideas to bubble up spontaneously

> Put yourself in positions or situations where **change** is needed—Artisans are masters at navigating the chaos that is often associated with transformation

- Remember that you are a problem solver and someone who likes to see new possibilities

- You activate flow for others, help people break out of old paradigms of thinking and help teams or projects get "unstuck" when you're at your best

- Other people may react and accuse you of not being

satisfied since you often want something new—you know change is needed for evolution; do notice when change is really needed vs. when you're simply feeling cranky

> Develop a healthy ability to **rebel, challenge** and poke holes in strategies or projects when you see something better is possible—Artisans crave elegant and sublime solutions and pursue them
  - Choose projects and teams where creative improvements are wanted
  - Learn to challenge in a way that is productive and in which others benefit as a result
  - Be aware when it might seem like you are complaining too much or are too attached to acting as a devil's advocate on the team—Artisans who do this can be disruptive and undermine progress that is valuable

> **Utilize other Talents** as your business grows—Artisans love the entrepreneurial stages and often lose their momentum and motivation in later stages
  - When it's time to scale the business, implement structure, create consistent and replicable processes in the business, and focus on efficiency—bring others in who enjoy this and are good at it
  - Keep in mind that starting and growing something new is exciting for an Artisan, but other Talents enjoy, and are often better at, creating conditions for long-term sustainability

> Trust that you'll have abundant **creative bursts** (as well as what appear to be lulls or less creative times)—Artisan energy

appears spontaneously and often in large blocks

- Don't make yourself wrong for having these cycles; they are part of your process
- If you can trust this creative flow, you can be fluid about what you do and don't get done at a micro level compared to the macro scope of all you accomplish

> If you can, **avoid** reporting to people who like **micromanagement**—Artisans rebel against control, so this style is often a lose-lose situation

- Micromanagement can disrupt your ability to find a productive rhythm and follow-through that is effective and authentic for you
- If you are reporting to someone who tends to micromanage, explore ways to negotiate for both of you getting what you want—if you can promise reliable results and your manager can give you room to accomplish those results in your own way within a reasonable time frame, this process will support a win-win

> Following **what you want** is important—Artisans can seem negative, focusing on what they don't want

- Looking for and putting your attention on what you want will increase your energy, attention and even follow-through
- Where you don't feel energy and motivation, see if you can delegate that activity
- Because Artisans are about pleasure and following what is pleasurable for them, it is important to lean toward what you want to do and to say no to what you don't want to do,

even if it may seem selfish

- If Artisans spend a lot of time and energy doing what they don't want to do, this can lead to crankiness and sabotage
- It's better, as an Artisan, for you to be honest when you're saying yes or no—this will ultimately serve others because you will be fully present and engaged when you say yes

TIPS & COACHING: WORKING WITH AN ARTISAN

If you discover you are managing or working with someone who has the Artisan Sweet Spot:

> Allow them to have **options and choices**—Artisans don't work well when they are fenced in

- When you give an Artisan no choice and no options, it only invites rebellion

> **Include them in brainstorming** conversations—Artisans enjoy it and are great at it

- This also supports them to buy-in with ideas that are proposed

> Listen to their **ideas**—Artisans have an unending flow of them

- They have great suggestions—use some
- They'll feel heard and less rebellious
- Let them know you have heard their ideas and that you appreciate them offering those ideas, even if you aren't going to execute them
- Don't assume that when they mention an idea that they'll

necessarily follow through on it—sometimes they are merely exploring

- Ask Artisans to help you solve problems when you're stuck

> Provide time and space for **percolation** and **bursts of results**—Artisans provide the best results when schedules and workspaces are open

- Artisans rarely work on others' time frames—be flexible
- Ask for results and give Artisans room to tell you how they see they can best achieve those results in a time frame that is realistic
- Encourage Artisans to design their workspaces in ways that inspire them—likely color, music, natural light and so on

> Encourage them to **simplify**, focus on what they most want and take steps toward it—complexity can overwhelm them and clog their creative process

- Artisans like choices but can get overwhelmed with possibilities and options
- Encourage them to take small steps toward what they want; this will build their confidence

> Encourage them **to say no** to what they don't want *AND* to propose alternative solutions—providing alternative solutions helps colleagues appreciate them

- It's powerful for Artisans to develop a muscle for saying no, because this means that when they say yes, they'll really mean it
- Proposing alternative solutions encourages them to take ownership of the situation and work toward success

FAMOUS ARTISANS

Alan Alda	Elvis Presley	Malcolm Gladwell
Albert Einstein	Gary Burghoff	Meg Ryan
Ashton Kutcher	Goldie Hawn	Michael Jackson
Bill Gates	Harry Houdini	Paul McCartney
Charles Lindbergh	Ho Chi Minh	Prince
Charlie Sheen	Humphrey Bogart	Robin Williams
Chris Rock	Isadora Duncan	Ron Howard
Cynthia Nixon	Jackie Chan	Spike Lee
David Carradine	John F. Kennedy Jr.	Stan Laurel
Dido	Jim Henson	Stephen Hawking
Don Adams	Jimi Hendrix	Steve Jobs
Drew Barrymore	Jodi Foster	Timothy Geithner
Dustin Hoffman	Lisa Kudrow	Tom Hanks
Eddie Murphy	Madonna	Yul Brynner

CHAPTER 2

THE PRIEST

CHRIS, VICE PRESIDENT OF PROJECT MANAGEMENT

Day of GlobalApp's corporate retreat:

It's 9:00 a.m., and I'm ready to start the conversation. I'm incredibly disappointed that we lost a key client—a client I had worked with every step of the way—and I'm getting antsy to open up a dialogue about what happened. I do think we have a solid group of leaders here, and I know our product has awesome potential to go big. I'm pretty optimistic that getting everyone talking together today can make a difference, maybe change the whole game, if people can get real with each other.

Right before the meeting, Lisa told the rest of us that she is doing fine; yet, I know she's upset that her current staff is underperforming and is stressing about it. "Lisa," I say, "why don't you just tell them the truth—that your staff stinks...you're not getting what you want from your staff and you're stuck?!" People are still sitting in the uncomfortable silence of that one, but I'm used to it now. There are certain things I've learned about getting people to be more authentic in meetings like this. If they think you are for them, they might go there; if they think you are not on their side, forget it.

Now it's apparently time for us to go around and answer the question that has been posed to us. "All right, Chris," Brian says, "you're up. What do you think is the biggest problem GlobalApp has?"

"Lack of vision," I say. "That's what it all boils down to. All in all, I believe GlobalApp has lost touch with what matters most. That's what is at the heart of why we lost a key client. Our developers seem to be too enamored with their own brilliance versus solving real problems for the clients, our leadership doesn't take enough ownership of the bigger company issues, and our employees aren't motivated or inspired because they are emotionally disconnected from what we're really building here—and, by the way, I am as well."

I get the sense that there are people in the room that think all this "vision" and "emotional commitment" talk is just a bunch of "soft" stuff. Part of me is totally disgusted and deflated, and part of me wonders if I am still making any kind of difference here....

What contribution is Chris making, and what unique value does he bring?

What is Chris overly focused on or attached to that is causing frustration?

THE PRIEST'S CONTRIBUTIONS

> You must find the place inside yourself
> where nothing is impossible.
> *Deepak Chopra*

Priests are typically all about **vision** and what they see as **the potential of human beings**. They can see beyond what is to what could be, and they often find that when people don't bridge the gap between current reality and future possibility, it can be frustrating and even painful to them. Priests can also see deeply into the people around them, beyond the surface appearance into who they really are and what they truly feel. Priests do not tend to play in shallow waters but crave deep connection with others, and they are acutely aware of any emotional inauthenticity or incongruence. They often bristle when people don't walk their talk. Natural leaders, Priests can be wonderful coaches, mentors, therapists and motivational speakers, inspiring us to move toward a greater purpose or to reach our own potential.

Priests usually have a **big, inspired vision**, seeing opportunities that can transform the world and those around them for the better. Whereas some people might focus on problems, limitations and obstacles, Priests can clearly see **possibilities** and feel motivated to find solutions. In the 1850s, most political rhetoric was based on the sanctity of the Constitution, a Constitution that tolerated slavery. In contrast, Abraham Lincoln emphasized the Declaration of Independence as the basis of the nation, which shifted the entire debate about slavery. In the 272 words and three minutes of his Gettysburg Address, Lincoln proclaimed that the nation was born in 1776, not 1789, and that it was "conceived in Liberty, and dedicated to the proposition that all men are created equal." He believed at a core level that human beings had the innate potential to see the truth about equality. Before Lincoln, many talked about simply ending slavery, but Lincoln was the first to emphasize the more far-reaching and inspiring concept that all humans are created equal—a radical view at the time.

Similarly, Evangelical preacher Billy Graham's vision saw far beyond the religious divisions of the Protestant church. Though theologically conservative, Graham consistently refused to be sectarian like other fundamentalists. From the beginning of his ministry in the 1940s, he emphasized inclusivity, embracing the then new media technologies, especially radio and television, to spread the gospel in a nonexclusive way. In fact, in later years, Graham was denounced as an "antichrist" when he stated his expansive vision as such: "I think that everybody that loves or knows Christ, whether they are conscious of it or not, they are members of the body of Christ…[God] is calling people out of the world for his name, whether they come from the Muslim world, or the Buddhist world or the non-believing world, they are members of the Body of Christ because they have been called by God. They may not know the name of Jesus but they know in their hearts that they need something they do not have, and they turn to the only light they have, and I think that they are saved and they are going to be with us in heaven."

> Heroes are ordinary men and women who dare to see and meet the call of a possibility bigger than themselves. Breakthroughs are created by such heroes, by men and women who will stand for the result while it is only a possibility—people who will act to make possibility real.
>
> *Werner Erhard*

Priests, inspired by the vision they see, can be skilled **motivators**. They tend to be **emotionally intelligent** and able to engage, uplift and align others to a vision. Jesse Jackson has worked relentlessly to align African Americans and others to his vision of equal rights using both his emotional intellect and his skills as a motivator. Jon Margolis of the *Chicago Tribune* noted that "more than most politicians, Jackson really engages the intellect. His basic appeal is more emotional than cerebral, based less on what he says than on the picturesque (and sometimes outrageous) way he says it. But what he says is often striking." As far as his ability to motivate, Robert Borosage, senior adviser to Jackson in his 1988 campaign, observed that Jackson "has an ability to reduce political discourse to one powerful, lyrical, narrative that both entertains and inspires. Words to him are like clay to a skilled potter; raw material which he effortlessly and deftly manipulates to mold, shape and define something of aesthetic as well as practical value." Jackson's skills as a motivator have uplifted countless numbers of people to participate in civil rights movement protests as well as his Rainbow/PUSH Coalition.

Abraham Lincoln, a skilled orator like many Priests, was famous for motivating the country through his inspiring writings and speeches, but he also had the emotional intelligence to time his public statements to get the emotional response he sought. He delayed announcing the Emancipation Proclamation until the Union achieved victory at the Battle of Antietam. Lincoln waited for this critical Union military victory to publish the Proclamation at a time he felt his troops and citizens would be most open to inspiration. He didn't want to appear desperate. Rather, he knew the power of motivating people from strength, the experience of "winning" and overcoming adversity, and chose his words and timing well to build on heightened emotions and positive beliefs.

Priests are often dedicated to promoting **growth** and encouraging **transformation**, for themselves, those around them and, ultimately, the world. A prime example of this quality is Werner Erhard, personal growth trainer and creator of the est training (which is now Landmark Education), who studied a multitude of spiritual disciplines, philosophies and authors who wrote about human potential. In the early 1970s, he brought the entire package together to create a popular and highly successful training program for growth and transformation on a scale not previously seen. Though controversial, Erhard's est training was one of the first intensive consciousness seminars of the human potential movement, the prototype for hundreds of spin-offs and workshops offered today. Erhard's vision was to "make the world work for everyone, with nobody left out," and he dedicated his life to promoting this type of transformational work.

In his commitment to the growth and transformation of victimized people, Jesse Jackson wrote, "People who are victimized may not be responsible for being down, but they must be responsible for getting up. Slave masters don't retire; people who are enslaved change their minds and choose to join the abolitionist [antislavery] struggle...Change has always been led by those whose spirits were bigger than their circumstances...I do have hope. We have seen significant victories during the last 25 years." Jackson dedicated his life to the growth of the human spirit and the transformation of people from being oppressed to being empowered.

> Never look down on anybody
> unless you're helping him up.
> *Jesse Jackson*

Priests often have the unique capacity for **seeing opportunities** for growth and **finding meaning** within the most difficult circumstances or situations. Actor/activist Angelina Jolie says that she initially set out to explore the world because she wanted to become a better person and to simply educate herself. But as she encountered refugees and disaster survivors in war-torn regions, she discovered more than she expected. "I've learned about family and just respect them so much and have seen so many horrible things and seen so much survival and so much beauty in these people. So they've changed my life." In response, over the past decade, Jolie was not only inspired to rescue several children from dire circumstances by adopting them, but she has donated millions of dollars and has become the spokesperson for numerous aid organizations. "When I found I could be useful in communicating what I had learned and maybe inspire other people to educate themselves and do some good, it made me so happy and gave me a sense of purpose." Jolie took an awful situation and saw the opportunity to make a difference and inspire others to do the same. She not only created an exponential impact in the world, she also did so within herself.

Deepak Chopra, author and holistic health advocate, publicly spreads his message that people can expand their capacity to recognize opportunities that were previously unseen. "Once you understand the way life really works—the flow of energy, information, and intelligence that directs every moment—then you begin to see the amazing potential in that moment." He contends that we can also find profound meaning not only in difficult situations, but also in what seem to be mundane situations or simple "coincidences." Chopra states, "When you live your life with an appreciation of coincidences and their meanings, you connect with the underlying field of infinite possibilities. This is when the magic begins."

Former secretary of state Condoleezza Rice saw the challenges facing the United States in 2005 as an opportunity to spread her idealistic view of US values that she felt would result in positive growth for all of humanity. "Our work has only begun. In our time we have an historic opportunity to shape a global balance of power that favors freedom and that will therefore deepen and extend the peace. And I use the word power broadly, because even more important than military and indeed economic power is the power of ideas, the power of compassion, and the power of hope."

....

I am not bound to win, but I am bound to

be true. I am not bound to succeed, but

I am bound to live by the light that I have.

I must stand with anybody that stands right,

and stand with him while he is right, and part

with him when he goes wrong.

Abraham Lincoln

....

Priests are typically committed to full **authenticity** within themselves, in their relationships and in their work. They sense when
they or others are out of **alignment with who they really are** and
seek to reestablish and maintain that alignment at all costs. In an
interview with Katie Couric, Condoleezza Rice said, "…don't let
anyone determine what your horizons are going to be. You get to
determine those yourself…and if you let others define who you
ought to be, or what you ought to be because they put you in a
category, they see your race, they see your gender and they put
you in a category. You shouldn't let that happen." In response to
why she would not run as presidential candidate Mitt Romney's
VP, Rice demonstrated her commitment to staying aligned with
who she is, despite the political opportunity, and stated, "I'm saying there is no way that I will do this, because it's really not me. I
know my strengths…."

Authors and personal growth leaders Kathlyn and Gay Hendricks
see authenticity as one of the cornerstones of their work. While

being filmed for *48 Hours* on CBS, Gay admitted to Kathlyn that he'd been having sexual fantasies about a former girlfriend. The TV producer was shocked and asked Kathlyn if she really needed to hear that, especially in public. She responded, "I'd much rather live in a world where people reveal themselves than in one where we conceal ourselves." They've used this philosophy to create their nonprofit Foundation for Conscious Living, an "organization committed to embodied Authenticity, Response-Ability, and Appreciation in partnership, community, politics, society, and the planet…[to create] a world in which everyone enjoys a flow of appreciation and co-creation, in an evolutionary (instead of fear-based) context."

When Werner Erhard was selected to contribute to Harvard University's *The Handbook for Teaching Leadership: Knowing, Doing, and Being*, he and the other authors insisted that "integrity, authenticity, and being committed to something bigger than oneself form the base of the context for leadership." To Erhard, authenticity leads to natural leadership and is defined as "being and acting consistent with who you hold yourself out to be for others, and who you hold yourself out to be for yourself."

> Love is granting another the space to be the way they are and the way they are not.
> *Werner Erhard*

Priests do not often shy away from the **truth**. They tend to **face what is real**, no matter how difficult, and insist that others do so as well. Dianne Feinstein refused to shy away from what she felt was an ugly truth about US torture and interrogation techniques. In her announcement about the controversial release of the CIA's report on the treatment of detainees, she stated, "America is big enough to admit when it's wrong and confident enough to learn from its mistakes." Against vitriolic criticism, Feinstein held firm in her belief that the United States needed to face what was going on and contended, "History will judge us by our commitment to a just society governed by law and the willingness to face an ugly truth and say: 'Never again.'"

> The truth will set you free,
> but first it will piss you off.
> *Gloria Steinem*

Journalist Barbara Walters was noted for her willingness to tell the truth in her interviews. Though she rarely alienated people she interviewed, she spoke with unusual boldness in stating what was real, once telling Muammar Gadhafi that Americans thought he was "mad" and another time confronting Fidel Castro regarding his definition of freedom. She often caught notables such as Margaret Thatcher, the Shah of Iran and Boris Yeltsin off guard, leading them to reveal more than they intended. She coached other interviewers to "wait for those unguarded moments. Relax the mood and, like the child dropping off to sleep, the subject often reveals his truest self." No matter how real, raw or controversial, Barbara was unafraid of truth-telling on her part or on the part of her subjects.

Priests tend to be **focused on what is fair**. As activist and actor Angelina Jolie declared, "I don't believe I feel differently from other people. I think we all want justice and equality, a chance for a life with meaning…."

Sharing his recent change in perspective on gay marriage, President Barack Obama explained, "Frankly, that's the kind of thing that prompts a change of perspective—not wanting to somehow explain to your child why somebody should be treated differently when it comes to [the] eyes of the law."

THE PRIEST UNDERBELLY

When pursuing their goals or their purpose, Priests can be **overly serious** and extremely **intense**, like a hungry dog after a bone. Barbara Walters, in her quest to promote serious journalism opportunities for women, demanded the title of cohost despite being paid half the salary of her counterpart. Through her tenacity, she became the first female coanchor of a news show and, years later, the highest-paid journalist in the United States. While this was a big win, it also earned her the rancor of her male colleagues.

Deep breaths are very helpful at shallow parties.
Barbara Walters

Priests can also be extremely **judgmental** and **self-righteous**, especially criticizing others for not stepping up to their potential.

Gary Younge of the *Guardian* noted that working with Jesse Jackson, who could be incredibly judgmental and self-righteous, was not easy. According to Younge, a former colleague of Jackson's stated that "he has a complete inability to trust anyone who works beneath him and at times that does become a real problem." A former advisor of Jackson's said that he "can be hugely insensitive. He can say and do things, almost without thinking, that are just terrible. Jackson loves humanity; it is people he has a problem with."

Without pain, there would be no suffering, without suffering we would never learn from our mistakes. To make it right, pain and suffering is the key to all windows, without it, there is no way of life.
Angelina Jolie

In Barbara Walters's famous interview with Monica Lewinsky, Walters asked, "What will you tell your children when you have them?" Lewinsky replied, "Mommy made a big mistake," at which point Walters responded, "And that is the understatement of the year."

This harsh judgment can also be turned inward, leading Priests to flagellate themselves, as in the case of the teenaged Angelina Jolie: "I collected knives and always had certain things around. For some reason, the ritual of having cut myself and feeling the pain, maybe feeling alive, feeling some kind of release, it was somehow therapeutic to me."

Unevolved Priests can sometimes **project their emotions** on others. They can become **overly dramatic** and **manipulative**, using emotions as a weapon. As a young man, Abraham Lincoln told his schoolteacher that he often contemplated suicide, and, as an older adult, he often wept in public and recited maudlin poetry.

Priests tend to be **perfectionists**, finding themselves and others never quite good enough. Singer Beyoncé rehearsed the national anthem during the presidential inauguration until her feet bled. But because she could not rehearse with the orchestra and get a proper sound check, she opted to sing with one of her prerecorded tracks. "I did not feel comfortable taking the risk. It was about the president and the inauguration, and I wanted to make him and my country proud."

Oh, God, I struggle with low self-esteem all the time! I think everyone does. I have so much wrong with me, it's unbelievable!
Angelina Jolie

Prior to finding their purpose, Priests may **overemphasize their sexuality**, often engaging in dangerous sexual activity. In contrast to her public persona, Jackie Kennedy was sexually sophisticated, displaying illustrations from the Kama Sutra in the dining room of one of her country houses. According to one biographer, Kennedy loved the game of seducing men, whether they were married or not. Angelina Jolie had a live-in boyfriend by the age of 14 and was married twice by the time she was 25. During that time, she projected a dangerous sexuality and even wore a vial of one husband's blood around her neck.

OTHER PRIEST CHARACTERISTICS

Priests can become fixated on the vision they see and ignore any other input or ideas. Early in their paths, Priests can be ungrounded and theoretical, ineffective at making their visions tangible. Their quest for perfection can make them narrow-minded, viewing the world as only black and white, good or bad, with no shades of gray. They are most attuned to their own feelings, thoughts and judgments and may discount the feelings, thoughts and judgments of others. Priests are also quite intuitive; they may not know how they know, but they are certain of what they know.

....

> These days my greatest teacher
> is my own inner silence.
> *Deepak Chopra*

....

Priests can be **impatient** as they view the gap between what could be (and in their minds, what should be) and what currently is. They feel **urgent** about fulfilling their purpose and, in their need for forward momentum, may push others too hard and prematurely. Priests are **passionate** and experience their emotions deeply and fully. They live in **Technicolor**, big and alive, and feel lost without a purpose that is large enough for the energy that runs through them. They are drawn to **spirituality** and **global thinking and action**.

PRIEST STAGES OF DEVELOPMENT

STAGE 1: Priests in Stage 1 tend to be hypercritical. Though they see what could be, or should be, their main focus is on what isn't, how people and systems are lacking and wrong. Their judgments are harsh and unyielding, and Priests at this stage can be aggressive and adamant about expressing their opinions. The result is that, rather than motivating others to step into their own potential and move toward expanded possibility, these Priests drag down those around them. This harsh criticism is also applied to themselves as they consistently fall short of the perfection they aspire to.

Stage 1 Priests can also be highly and uncontrollably emotional, but unlike the ever-changing emotionality of an Artisan, Priests' emotions run deep and are often dark—leading to intense, lasting despair. Because Priests are so good at sensing the emotions of others, they can be emotionally manipulative, using their knowledge to get what they want by appealing to what they can sense the person is lacking or attached to.

Priests in Stage 1 can be coached to change their focus—to begin to look for the positive rather than only the negative and what's right rather than what's wrong in people, situations and especially in themselves. Rather than directing their focus on how current conditions are lacking, Stage 1 Priests will benefit by accepting "what is" simply as a starting point and focusing on how to move toward the possibilities they see so clearly. If they refuse, ask them if they really want the other person to change. Priests who do this will find themselves becoming more optimistic and productive.

STAGE 2: Priests at Stage 2 can be grim and overly intense, taking themselves and their visions quite seriously. But now they are more in control of their emotions, and, though they still tend to be dramatic, they will tone down their reactions to better match and meet those they are engaging. These Priests are still inclined to judge people and situations as right or wrong, black or white, and fair or unfair—setting up a polarity of good versus bad. However, now they are more focused on the possibilities for the future they see and the potentials of people around them they perceive. In fact, Stage 2 Priests often idealize and overemphasize these possibilities and potentials, becoming fanatical in their devotion to "what could be" and "what should be." They often become perfectionists.

Priests in this stage can be extraordinarily impatient, feeling an urgency to see their visions manifest; yet, these Priests are not yet grounded and are often described as lots of talk and little action. These Priests see huge possibilities, so they can be overwhelmed and frustrated by their own inability to move tangibly toward them. In response, some Stage 2 Priests will channel their frustrated energies into sexuality.

Because Priests are so attuned to emotions, it is important that they do their own emotional work to understand themselves and ground themselves. They can also be encouraged to determine the specific impact they want to make and choose how and when to attempt to inspire others by first getting clear about who is ready and who is not. To broaden their perspectives on right versus wrong and fair versus unfair, ask them to explore how they know when something is fair, as opposed to thinking they mysteriously can tell when it is and isn't. Ask them how they can be okay themselves when someone doesn't take their coaching or advice. Priests who can let go of being everyone's coach and being the authority on fairness will be calmer and better able to make conscious choices. They will be more spacious with others and will be more aware of their impact on others before acting.

STAGE 3: Priests at this stage are beginning to manifest their visions. They are able to inspire others, pulling them with motivation rather than pushing them via criticism or fear. These Priests have become uplifters rather than downdraggers, and others around them feel seen and deeply understood. Stage 3 Priests are emotionally authentic and are able to perceive and elicit that same authenticity from others.

Stage 3 Priests are clearer about the steps between "what is" and "what will be," and they are willing to, and do, take those steps. They are realizing that all steps count, even if they are small. They remain passionate about growth and expansion, but, at this stage, they have developed more patience for the natural unfolding of their visions. These Priests are beginning to trust their own intuition and inner wisdom without requiring others to agree with them. The excess energy they once channeled into sexuality is now focused toward a sense of spirituality and purpose. They have learned emotional awareness—how to accept their own emotions, be with them and use them to create more engagement and connection. The more they connect authentically with themselves, the more they get the connection they want with others.

Priests in Stage 3 are becoming more authentic themselves and modeling authenticity for others. By Stage 3, Priests have begun to come into their own and offer their unique gifts, and they may develop even larger visions at this stage. These Priests can be supported by understanding the importance of alone time or quiet time to tap their own inner resources and awareness. It's also critical that they understand that, though they are inspiring uplifters, they are not responsible for the growth or transformation of those who seek them out. They'll be most successful when they primarily focus on the easy paths to uplift themselves while secondarily uplifting and inspiring others.

STAGE 4: Priests at this stage are aware that their pure presence and strong connection to the group's vision is their biggest contribution. These Priests have a sense of peace and spaciousness about them, exuding a deep trust in the perfect unfolding of people, processes and projects. Their visions are global and large in scope, and they maintain a broad spiritual awareness of how each piece, person and action fits into the universal whole.

PRIEST SWEET SPOT—KEY POINTS

VALUES

- vision, building a meaningful future, people's potential
- insight, intuition, spirituality
- being real, truth-telling, deep conversations
- passion, emotional intelligence, self-awareness, presence
- living authentically and with purpose, walking the talk
- growth, transformation, inspiration, motivation
- fairness

TRIGGERS

- avoiding the truth
- emotional incongruence
- playing small, not stepping up to reach potential
- lack of commitment or alignment

CHALLENGES

- drama, projecting emotions on others
- intensity, impatience
- being judgmental and righteous, black-and-white thinking, moral arrogance
- fixating on their vision, judging, criticizing, should-ing
- demanding perfection of themselves and others

GREAT ORGANIZATIONAL ROLES

- executive, group leader, project manager or project lead
- promoting a cause, making an impact, environmental stewardship
- coach, therapist

- trainer, teacher (educational, spiritual)

THE PRIEST LEADER
- keeps an eye on the big picture
- brings everything back to the vision and the "why"
- brings truths to the surface so the group can authentically dialogue, align, and feel motivated and bought-in
- empowers other leaders

TIPS & COACHING: LEVERAGING YOUR PRIEST TALENT

If you discover you've got the Priest Sweet Spot while reading this chapter, these are ways you can experience the most joy, ease and collaboration and create the best results:

> Build a strong sense of **purpose** in your work and ensure you're aligned with the mission and vision of projects you contribute to—Priests can't get behind things they don't believe in
- Check in to see how much you believe in the organizations, projects and people that you work with so you do things that **engage your passion**—if you don't, you are likely to lose motivation or, even worse, sabotage things
- You're likely to experience more energy when you're inspired, so find a cause to support, be in a position to help others grow, build and develop a team, manage a big project, bring transformation to an area or issue, engage a spiritual purpose, etc.
- When you're not aligned with something, **speak your truth**

about it in the most healthy and constructive way possible—not revealing your authentic perspective and feelings will only sabotage things later

> Take quiet time to **connect with yourself**—when a Priest is present to their deep emotional knowing, confusion clears, solutions appear and everything seems to just "line up"

- Take a walk around the block or in nature, sit quietly in your office with the door closed for five to ten minutes—be with yourself, take a few full breaths and listen for what's really true for you
- Give yourself moments to pause in a conversation, take space when you need it and connect with what you think and feel; don't fill all the empty space in your life!

> Know and presence your **vision**—the big picture is important to a Priest so they know how all the pieces fit together to build the whole

- Focus on your overall outcome to ensure everything you do and your team does is on purpose (or you'll likely doubt, won't feel motivated and won't clearly see what there is to do next)
- Take time and space to explore and clarify your vision for your own success—on a project, in your business, with your team or in a relationship
- You contribute by helping others articulate and focus on their vision—ask, "How would you like to feel when you accomplish your goals? What do you imagine success will look like in the future? What are you inspired about as you

look into the future?"

> **Celebrate progress**—Priests can get overly focused on the gap between now and where they want to be, which tightens them and slows things down

- Appreciate your own and other people's progress; it empowers everyone to take steps toward a bigger future
- Ask others, "What progress do you feel good about—that you've made or helped others make? What results have you achieved since we last talked? What are a few next steps you could take toward the bigger goals?"
- Focus on what is working to fuel your journey and propel yourself and others forward

> **Be patient** with the unfolding process, the growth process— Priests often focus on the outcome and get impatient with the process (which then sabotages forward movement)

- Provide value by helping people connect to their vision; however, don't inadvertently beat others up about the gap between where they are now and where they're headed
- Explore how you can focus on and appreciate the learning that the journey offers—help others enjoy the power of this journey (and its benefits) as well
- Apply this to yourself—feel some of the appreciation, celebration and patience you give to others

> Develop the skill to **know and own your feelings**—Priests are good at reading people emotionally, but if they don't know their own feelings, they falsely imagine that others feel what they feel (i.e., project their feelings)

- Recognize how you experience the core feelings of sad, mad, glad, scared and sexual (similar to the concept of primary colors) in your body and practice noticing them in the moment (e.g., anger often appears in the jaw, head, neck, shoulders and back)
- Recognizing your feelings will support you in taking responsibility for them
- Practice experiencing the wave of feelings inside yourself and also wisely expressing how you feel in a simple way that moves things forward—this is a great demonstration for others and helps you distinguish between what is really yours and what is not yours

> **See what's real in the present moment** in addition to what's possible—Priests can focus on potential and unknowingly sabotage progress

- Recognize the gap between what could be and what is here now so that you engage people where they are—meet others and inspire them to take real steps forward with the capacity they have available (just engaging another's potential can leave them feeling shamed and you frustrated)
- When you're leading a person or group of people you want to move forward, ask questions so that they discover, in their own words, what they are ready for and really willing to do (otherwise you might encourage them to take a step that is too big, setting them up to fail)
- Notice signals from others that you are going too big—their voices might get higher; they may move back from the table; they may get stiff and look away—don't bypass this feedback

- Be watchful to notice if you idealize a vision or future you can see—when you get attached to something that isn't realistic, no one will be able to join you, and, ultimately, you'll fail or slow progress (this is particularly risky when idealizing people—it sets you up to be frustrated and disappointed with them later; attempt to see people as they are now)

TIPS & COACHING: WORKING WITH A PRIEST

If you discover you are managing or working with someone who has the Priest Sweet Spot:

> Give a Priest both **people and projects to lead, inspire and grow**—this energizes and motivates them
  - Help them to frame or view their work within the context of leadership or about growing and inspiring people as much as possible—this is enlivening to a Priest
  - Encourage them to create goals that require them to step into their own potential and to be purposeful in their work
  - Suggest the Priest create individual goals that are related to improving the group's teamwork, effectively mentoring or coaching others, managing a project to client expectations, etc.
  - If the Priest that works for you is focused primarily on small details or sitting behind a computer with little to no interaction with people, help them shift some time and attention to include some bigger picture conversations and

more real-time human interaction

> Help your Priest build a vision that is inspiring to them, and then encourage them to **get on the ground with it now**—even if only with **small steps**

- Once they have created a picture of success that they feel emotionally connected to, support them in creating simple next steps and taking action (small steps can lead to big change over time; they may want to take steps that are too big)
- If they describe a future possibility that is too big for others, remind them to "walk their talk" and "think global, act local" so that others get a realistic demonstration of what's possible
- Invite them to keep bringing the vision forward if others forget it—ask them to share the bigger picture on a regular basis (be prepared that they might bring the vision back up with some fervor if others have gone off course)

> Reflect back how **their contribution** provides value—share how they've made a difference

- Share with them how their leadership, whether formal or informal, supports you and the team—specifically appreciate them for encouraging you and others to expand and stretch into potential
- Appreciate Priests for the direct impact they have; point out to them how they support healthier group dynamics, move meetings or projects forward, facilitate more candid dialogue, etc.

- Have them get direct feedback from the people they contribute to (colleagues, clients, etc.) since Priests do best when they hear directly from the people they're impacting—they'll experience the rich emotional overtones and undertones this way (and, at a minimum, pass on indirect feedback you hear)

> **Honor their feelings and experience**—never tell a Priest how they feel or coach them without permission
  - Don't overstep or invalidate how a Priest feels—particularly when something seems incongruent or out of alignment to them
  - If you accidentally tell a Priest how they might feel, they'll be sure to let you know—apologize and start over
  - Reflect back what you hear and sense they are feeling without trying to fix them
  - Directly ask and wait to hear that a Priest wants your coaching and feedback before you give it, or you'll only make a challenging situation worse
  - Encourage them to take time to check in to find and listen to their own inner wisdom or intuition

> **Be real** with them—have authentic conversations
  - Share how you feel, your concerns and desires, and so on, or the Priest may have trouble connecting with and listening to you—when in doubt, go deep
  - Don't avoid problems; face the mess—Priests relax when people face the truth
  - Schedule times to meet with the Priest when you can be

fully present (e.g., no multitasking), especially in the case of a performance review or when you have an important topic to discuss

> Ask and encourage them to **celebrate progress**—seeing the glass as half full rather than half empty is more inspiring

- Help the Priest recognize what *IS* working; this fuels their and other's motivation to keep growing and moving forward
- Remind the Priest to celebrate their own progress too! (Priests can be particularly hard on themselves)

FAMOUS PRIESTS

Angelina Jolie	Halle Berry	Mary Baker Eddy
Barack Obama	Hillary Clinton	Mary Tyler Moore
Barbara Walters	Jackie Kennedy	Nancy Pelosi
Beyoncé	James Brown	Omar Sharif
Bryant Gumbel	Jennifer Aniston	Ravi Shankar
Byron Katie	Jesse Jackson	Robert Pattison
Condoleezza Rice	Joan Borysenko	Rod Sterling
Deepak Chopra	Johnny Mathis	Sai Maa
Dianne Feinstein	Julia Roberts	Sandra Bullock
Faith Hill	Ken Wilber	Sarah Palin
Francois Mitterrand	Maria Shriver	Shri Anandi Ma
Gangaji	Marianne Williamson	Sir Edmond Hilary
Geena Davis	Mark Harmon	Thomas Gibson
Gloria Steinem	Martina Navratilova	Whitney Houston

CHAPTER 3

THE SAGE

DAVE, VICE PRESIDENT OF SALES

Day of GlobalApp's corporate retreat:

I'm not quite sure why Brian didn't ask me to run this meeting. I think he's one of the most brilliant guys out there, but he can't always capture a group's attention quite the way I can. Connecting with everyone over breakfast was something that was sorely needed, and I feel good coming into this meeting. It's a great opportunity to get everyone's input, to get people speaking the same language and start acting like a team.

I'm generally of the opinion that being overly serious and critical never seems to get us anywhere, but I'm pretty upset about losing this particular client. I put a lot of work into building that relation-ship. These are people I golfed with, vacationed with—I consider these people my friends. I'm mad that they didn't think to call me and embarrassed that I didn't know what was going on. My ego is a little bruised, but, more importantly, it's a relationship I value that is now a mess, and I don't know if I can clean it up. I'm also wondering what kind of impact this will have on future referrals.

This is not good.

Kevin showed up to the meeting right before it started and didn't join us for breakfast. That ticks me off. How are we going to be a successful team if we don't spend time together? I mean, that's when conversation really happens.

We've started going around the table, and now Brian has asked for my input on what GlobalApp's biggest problem is. "Lack of communication and collaboration," I boom. "We need to talk more and get on the same team here. That way nothing gets stalled, and we know what's going on with our clients. Right now, everyone's operating in silos. We need to pick up the phone, people, and just talk! Communicate! Nothing's going to happen until we get that handled."

I go on a bit more until I get interrupted by Chris. This used to bother me, but I know I sometimes talk too much. What's bothering me now is that despite the talent in this room, they don't seem to get how important it is to talk as a team. Yankee Casey Stengel said it best: "Gettin' good players is easy. Getting 'em to play together is the hard part." There's no way I would leave Brian high and dry—our relationship is too tight—but it's starting to be a real drag and not as much fun as it used to be. And I know if I'm not having fun, clients will know it, and sales will suffer.

> What contribution is Dave making, and what unique value does he bring?
>
> What is Dave overly focused on or attached to that is causing frustration?

THE SAGE'S CONTRIBUTIONS

Sages are first and foremost about **communication**. They are typically the ones who say what we're thinking that we won't say out loud. They can connect us both to themselves and to each other. They have the ability to make life fun, bringing their exuberance and playfulness to everything they do and inviting us to do the same. With their earthiness and big appetites for life, Sages can show us how to savor our moments and add humor and fun to our everyday lives. Often brilliant speakers, comedians, politicians and entertainers, their infectious humor and knack for storytelling can be incredibly attractive. We simply feel better about our lives and ourselves in their presence.

> That's their role, to be the jester or the fool who says, "Let me talk about things you might not be talking about yourself and let me invite you into that conversation."
> *Jessica Halem*

As master **communicators**, Sages generally know how to capture our attention and make their communication **engaging and entertaining**. Award-winning broadcast journalist Walter Cronkite, known at one point as "the most trusted man in America," is a prime example of this masterful way of communication. When Cronkite covered lengthy presidential conventions in the '50s and '60s, most of his commentary had to be spontaneous. He is said to have "blazed like a meteor" as he demystified the political process for the American public, holding their rapt attention for up to seven hours at a time. A well-developed Sage's narration of events brings us right into the action and makes us feel part of the stories they tell. Sages don't just lay out the facts but can **paint vivid word portraits** for us so we come to a new understanding of events.

Cronkite was an expert in creating a vivid picture in the listener's mind, such as the time he described an air battle during World War II: "American Flying Fortresses have just come back from an assignment to hell—a hell of 26,000 feet above the earth, a hell of burning tracer bullets and bursting gunfire, of crippled Fortresses and burning German fighter planes, of parachuting men and others not so lucky."

> The only thing we have to fear is fear itself.
> *Franklin D. Roosevelt*

Sages can also be brilliant at **synthesizing their messages** through **expert use of language** to make sure their communication is **clear and meaningful**. First Lady Eleanor Roosevelt, described as intelligent and opinionated, was not content to stay in her husband's shadow and handle domestic duties. Determined to show the world that a first lady could be an important part of

American politics, she studied language, literature and history, and she learned to state her positions on controversial political events clearly and concisely. A *Time* magazine article reported of Roosevelt that, "like a good dinner hostess, she is able to dart into controversial subjects (birth control, Senator Joe McCarthy, racial segregation) and out again, getting her strong opinions across in a deceptively mild way." Unlike prior first ladies, Roosevelt gave her own press conferences and spoke out for human rights, children's causes and women's issues. She wrote a syndicated newspaper column that reached millions of Americans (published from 1935 to 1962) dealing with key events, controversial topics and social and political issues, subjects far out of the range of the conventional first lady's communications.

> My whole thing is to entertain, make people laugh and to forget about the real world for awhile.
> *Dan Aykroyd*

Sages also tend to love **humor**. They often have an instinctive funny bone that allows them to see the **irony** and comedy in everyday life that many of us miss. Using humor, Sages can say difficult things and **expose the elephant in the room** without alienating people. As Jay Leno put it, "You can't stay mad at someone who makes you laugh." Popular actor and comedian Ellen DeGeneres has exhibited Sage qualities throughout her career. She created a funny, awkward scene in her sitcom to come out publicly as a lesbian, and, in doing so, helped put the issue of same-sex partnerships on the national agenda. Despite the controversial nature of her views to certain segments of the population, she continues to be widely and wildly popular and a much sought-after product spokesperson. As one CEO put it, "I think Ellen is someone we all trust. She's lovable, likable, honest and funny, but at her soul, we trust her." Sage comedians have tackled some of society's most sensitive subjects with biting and outrageous humor. Although they are not loved by all, few can deny that they are gifted in their abilities to bring light and acceptance to aspects of our culture people feel scared of and try to keep in the dark, all while making us laugh out loud about our humanity. Contributions from people like Mel Brooks, the Smothers Brothers, Dennis Miller and many others have impacted public opinion and opened up dialogue in areas where fear often reigns.

Behind every great man is a woman rolling her eyes.

Jim Carrey

Sages are known to love life and all it has to offer. They can have **big appetites** for everything from sex to food. They often seek out and savor **joyful indulgence** and are often described as **living large**. Songwriter and businesswoman Dolly Parton typifies this Sage quality. She has been rumored to have an open marriage with her husband of 45 years, and Carl Parton has never denied speculations about her affairs. Dolly's love of men seems to openly be a source of joy and living life to the fullest. "I love to flirt, and I've never met a man I didn't like," she claims. "Men are my weakness. Short, fat, bald or skinny—I've had crushes on some very unusual men but Carl knows I'll always come home." Parton also loves to eat and identifies potatoes and gravy as yet another one of her great passions in life.

> I can't do nothing just a little.
> *Dolly Parton*

Sages' love of good food can be a tremendous gift that allows everyone else to indulge as well. Celebrity chef Mario Batali brings his big appetite for life and love of food to people worldwide. "In the end," he says, "the only reason I am motivated to do what I do is for the hedonistic pleasures of the table."

When it comes to living large, Sage Jay Leno is another prime example. He is well-known for his indulgence in rare and spectacular cars, reportedly owning 286 vehicles (169 automobiles and 117 motorcycles).

> Life is a great big canvas;
> throw all the paint you can at it.
> *Danny Kaye*

Through their innate ability to sense how to draw people in and keep them connected, Sages can be gifted **community builders**, creating **interconnected networks**, often composed of people of disparate viewpoints and backgrounds. According to historian Douglas Brinkley, through Walter Cronkite, *CBS News* became "the meeting hall, the cathedral, the corner bar and the town square." During the height of his career, the entire nation felt connected to him. In fact, then-president Lyndon B. Johnson commented, "If I've lost Cronkite, I've lost the country."

> I am saddened by how people treat one another and how we are so shut off from one another and how we judge one another, when the truth is, we are all one connected thing. We are all from the same exact molecules.
>
> *Ellen DeGeneres*

Eleanor Roosevelt was also a magnet who drew people to her, from the US military men she visited in overseas hospitals and mess halls to the 15,000 Indians who clamored to greet her in Bombay. She specifically used her popularity to build and empower a strong network of women. She banned male reporters from her press conferences, requiring major publications to hire female reporters. Roosevelt worked to integrate qualified women into the Roosevelt administration and the federal government in high and midlevel administrative posts and successfully expanded the Civil Works Administration and the Federal Emergency Relief Administration to deal with problems specific to unemployed women.

Sages, when they use their gifts well, can also effectively build communities by staying in the background. For example, Garrison Keillor, who hosts and is intimately involved in just about every element of *A Prairie Home Companion*, receives no credit or billing, except as part of a joke or spoof.

Sages are often able to move things forward by moving within and creating a **flow**. Sages can be highly attuned to the **group flow and rhythm**, and they typically know how to help move a group forward if it becomes stuck in inertia. They often pay **attention to patterns** and, based on these patterns, they are aware of what is happening as it should and can pinpoint what isn't. The flow a Sage can create may also show up in the ability to synchronize different groups or loosen up individuals within a group to be more expressive and participatory.

Eleanor Roosevelt was acutely attuned to the organizational flow necessary to produce significant political results. Realizing that ideology alone did not win elections, she became a leading political figure in New York in the 1920s by redirecting women and reform groups to set goals that were realistic for the political climate, to prioritize tasks and schedule them to coincide with other significant events, and to coordinate with other groups to effectively achieve their aims. This resulted in a flow of people and resources that created a wildly successful campaign.

Everything is changing. People are taking the comedians seriously and the politicians as a joke.
Will Rogers

Comedian Ellen DeGeneres builds her audience community from the moment she steps on stage in her vest and tie, dancing with housewives from Indiana and street kids from Chicago. Her playful rapport allows her audience to remain cohesive and comfortable when she tackles controversial topics such as the online boycott launched by OneMillionMoms.com when she became a spokesperson for JC Penney.

THE SAGE UNDERBELLY

> How do I stay so healthy and boyishly handsome? It's simple. I drink the blood of young runaways.
> *William Shatner*

As delightful as Sages can be, they can be difficult in many ways. They **crave to be the center of attention** and show a fiercely **competitive** streak when they are not. In his biography about Walter Cronkite, David Brinkley wrote that Cronkite had a darker, competitive side and hated sharing the spotlight. Upon finding out he was to share the anchor desk with Edward R. Murrow, he locked himself in the anchor booth and refused to come out for publicity photos. As Tom Brokaw said, "He was very protective of his seat of power. This 'nicest guy in the world' was more Darwinian than you could imagine when it came to being top dog."

William Shatner, lead actor in the original *Star Trek* series, is also described by other actors as having a huge ego and said he often argued to have others' lines or close-ups cut so he could gain more airtime for himself. In an interview, George Takei, another actor on the original *Star Trek* series, states, "He's very self-possessed, self-involved, everything revolves around The Captain.

They may have been setting up a close-up on [another actor], because she's got the line but then he would take the director off to a dark corner and have a whispered conversation. And then the director comes back and moves the camera that way [to Shatner]." Of Shatner's film in which he interviews four different *Star Trek* captains, the *New York Times* says, "Much of the fun of watching *The Captains* is waiting to see just how shameless a huckster and self-promoter Mr. Shatner can be."

Sages have a propensity to **hate being interrupted** and will often simply **not shut up**. Enamored with their own voices, they may **overtalk** and actually obscure the points they are trying to make. Walter Cronkite's coverage of the 1964 Republican convention was so boring and wordy that the chairman of CBS yanked him off the broadcast.

Never use a big word when a little filthy one will do.
Johnny Carson

Sages can also relish their own storytelling or jokes so much that they may get carried away with themselves, at times becoming **inappropriate** or even **vulgar**. Radio personality Garrison Keillor has been known to slip tongue-in-cheek and inadvertently offensive remarks into his homespun monologues on *A Prairie Home Companion*, such as, "The country has come to accept stereotypical gay men—sardonic fellows with fussy hair who live in overdecorated apartments with a striped sofa."

Roseanne Barr crossed the line for many people when she

mocked singing the national anthem at a pro baseball game with an intentionally awful voice followed by spitting on the ground and making vulgar gestures, apparently thinking it would be funny to imitate the baseball players' crude behaviors. This did not go over well with the public and caused a national uproar and harsh criticism of Barr.

Things people say strike me as amusing, and I am prone to saying out loud what everybody's thinking.

William Shatner

Sages can also easily become **overly verbose** and **reveal more than they should**, as when Geraldo Rivera, then a war correspondent in Iraq, started drawing details of an upcoming army operation in the sand during a Fox News broadcast. Sages also have a tendency to **make up** what they say on the spot, which can sometimes be problematic. In one of his speeches in Tennessee, George W. Bush seemed to be operating off the cuff when he stated, "There's an old saying in Tennessee—I know it's in Texas, probably in Tennessee—that says, fool me once, shame on—shame on you. Fool me—you can't get fooled again." It went down as one of the top ten "Bushisms" online. Needless to say, Bush Jr.'s attempts to make something up on the spot generally did not go well for him.

Sages often appear **untrustworthy** because, to them, the **impact of their story is more important than the facts**. Walter Cronkite's first radio job was to broadcast college football games.

He read the plays off the ticker, and then reenacted them as if he were in the stadium, saying, "I didn't need any facts. I just used my imagination."

> I believe in looking reality straight
> in the eye and denying it.
> *Garrison Keillor*

Television personality Geraldo Rivera is famous for stories that are light on facts and heavy in drama, such as the time he reported that he was at the scene of a friendly fire incident during the Afghanistan war, when he was actually 300 miles away, or when he estimated a US satanic cult to have over one million followers when only ten thousand had ever been identified.

Similar to degrading the importance of facts, Sages can often get caught up in their story and have a penchant for overpromising and underdelivering. This again can cause a lack of trust and can be a source of frustration for people.

> I can get in front of an audience and be in control.
> I suppose it's manipulation. Offstage, I'm aloof
> because I'm not very comfortable.
> *Johnny Carson*

Sages may be prone to using their great persuasive abilities to **pressure others** into doing or feeling what they want them to do or feel. In his article, James Pfiffner asserted that George W. Bush pressured the United States to go to war with Iraq with reasoning that was "based on dubious evidence that was presented in a misleading manner" and that the US intelligence community may have been "under unusual pressure to support the administration's goal."

Sages can often let their **large appetites** get away from them and become **overly indulgent** in their pursuit of joyful gratification. Walter Cronkite was known to be a partier, letting loose in bars and dining with miniskirted go-go dancers. As Andy Rooney once wrote, "The greatest old master in the art of living that I know is Walter Cronkite. If life were fattening, Walter Cronkite would weigh 500 pounds."

Likewise, Orson Welles, the highly acclaimed film director and actor who cowrote, directed and starred in *Citizen Kane*, had a famously large appetite for food and women. An average dinner for Welles, whose weight ballooned to nearly 400 pounds at his heaviest, was said to be comprised of two rare steaks and a pint of scotch. His love of women led him into several marriages with extramarital affairs during most of them.

My doctor told me to stop having intimate dinners for four. Unless there are three other people.
Orson Welles

Musician and songwriter Elton John openly admits that he has battled addictions to drugs and alcohol for most of his career. His extravagant lifestyle—reportedly spending nearly $60 million in a

20-month period with $420,000 spent on flowers alone—includes four luxury homes, vintage cars, fine jewelry, high-end clothing and outrageous stage costumes and has created severe financial difficulties for John despite his massive earnings.

OTHER SAGE CHARACTERISTICS

Sages tend to build **strong relationships** with others. Within groups, they are aware of engaging everyone and **leaving no one out**, which helps form solid communities. Through their willingness to acknowledge the elephant in the room, Sages are able to **facilitate consensus-building** and dispel any silos that begin to form within a community.

Sages can insist that life be **fun**. They typically **avoid being overly serious** about anything, especially about themselves. Their playful nature allows others to loosen up and express themselves more freely. Sages are often earthy and grounded, aware of their physical environments as well as their own bodies. They can be **rhythmic** in their movements and often love to dance. Well-developed Sages have learned how to **use their bodies to access their awareness** of others, group flow and the next right actions to take.

> I always try to balance the light with the heavy—a few tears of human spirit in with the sequins and the fringes.
> *Bette Midler*

Ironically, though highly skilled Sages have become experts with group interaction, communication and language, they are often more **slow to develop** socially and verbally than other types.

I know this sounds strange, but as a kid,
I was really shy. Painfully shy.

Jim Carrey

SAGE STAGES OF DEVELOPMENT

STAGE 1: Sages in Stage 1 tend to be over-the-top in many ways. They love to talk but simply don't know when to stop and give the floor to others. Rather than having conversations, they create monologues that irritate those around them. Rather than drawing people in, this constant running of the mouth tends to push people away. Stage 1 Sages crave being the center of attention at all times and will do whatever it takes to get that attention, whether it's by being overly loud, inappropriate or vulgar.

Stage 1 Sages want everything to be fun and funny. When serious conversation or action is called for, they avoid it or even try to derail it using humor. Insatiable in their appetites, Sages at this stage constantly seek joy and play, which can become gluttony as they overindulge in food, parties, drugs or sex. They hate being alone and sometimes avoid self-reflection and deep thought.

Stage 1 Sages evolve as they get curious about how to have fun *with* others. With this focus, they begin to listen and pay closer attention to the responses they get. Their communications become more meaningful rather than constantly "performing" and being "on" in their interactions. Stage 1 Sages learn to soothe their hunger for attention by exploring how to give attention to themselves rather than always requiring it from others.

STAGE 2: Though they now allow themselves to be quiet and even serious at times, Sages at this stage can get so entertained by their own wordplay and flair for sophisticated language that they are still inclined to monopolize the conversation. Because they are so focused on showing off their verbal skills, Stage 2 Sages tend to lose the focus of the material they are delivering and obscure the points they are trying to make. Others can view them as boorish and confusing and avoid participating with them. These Sages continue to use humor to connect, but their humor can be edgy, sarcastic and shaming rather than inviting.

Stage 2 Sages still focus on themselves, but they are now interested in getting others to join in their interests and activities. Their persuasive abilities are great, but Sages at this stage can be very manipulative and not yet consistent in considering the needs and desires of those they seek to persuade. Though their stories are convincing, these Sages can be loose with the truth, sacrificing accuracy to make their stories more powerful and convincing. This makes them appear slippery and untrustworthy.

Sages in Stage 2 can be encouraged to continue to hone their listening skills to create more effective communications and engaging interactions. They can be coached to notice when enough is enough, whether it is in talking, being humorous or instigating play. These Sages are also ready to start considering the desires and well-being of others and to make sure that their persuasiveness is used for the good of all, and not just for their own gains.

STAGE 3: Sages in Stage 3 are coming into their own. They know how and when to listen, and they are more aware of and interested in those around them. This gives them the ability to become the mouthpiece for other's desires and intentions, not just their own. Rather than monopolizing all interactions, these Sages are now able to use their big, effusive energy to act as the social lubricant within the group to create flow and cohesiveness. They have become skilled at engaging others to participate. Now more sensitive to group dynamics and timing, these Sages are able to enhance forward movement and help prevent inertia.

Sages in this stage still enjoy a large appetite for life and pleasure, but they have learned a healthy balance. Their earthiness and vibrancy is magnetic, and their playful enthusiasm is infectious. These Sages have an attractive ease about them that makes others feel good just being in their presence. Stage 3 Sages are more attuned to the flow, rhythm and timing of communication and activity, and they are learning to use their bodies as a barometer for sensing group dynamics.

Stage 3 Sages can benefit from giving themselves even more time for silence and reflection to become more attuned to their inner sense of flow and rhythm. This allows them to increase their capacity to smoothly interact with others. They'll be most successful at engaging others when they consider what will be most fun and satisfying for everyone. They'll be most motivated by focusing on what's possible when groups are interconnected and in flow.

STAGE 4: Stage 4 Sages are fully comfortable in their own skin. They bring a delightful playfulness to life and now recognize that it is their presence, not their verbal skills, that gives the most value. These Sages have a clear sense of the rhythms, cycles and flows within groups and activities, and they use that sense to manifest their objectives with ease and grace. They facilitate groups forming and interconnecting. They listen deeply and encourage others to follow their own rhythm, to synchronize, to live a full life and to savor joy.

SAGE SWEET SPOT—KEY POINTS

CORE VALUES & BEHAVIORS
- communication, language
- being engaging, entertaining
- telling rich stories with metaphors and vivid images
- interconnected communities, inclusiveness, relationship building
- humor, fun, irony, exposing the elephant in the room
- interaction, flow, being attuned to group dynamics
- appetite—enjoying and savoring life

TRIGGERS

- seriousness, lack of fun
- group inertia—when the group is not in flow
- silos—communication and interaction not happening

CHALLENGES

- wanting to be the center of attention
- talking too much, too loud, too vulgarly, revealing too much
- willing to say anything, change the story or make stuff up "on the fly"
- pressuring others with persuasive language
- indulgent appetite—too much of a good thing

GREAT ORGANIZATIONAL ROLES

- sales and marketing
- leadership—team and coalition building
- client and customer engagement, community development
- culture messaging, internal communication

THE SAGE LEADER

- engages everyone, builds relationships, forms community
- creates playful and fun interactions with conversation and activities
- lightens up the mood to get things flowing
- speaks of any elephant in the room
- facilitates reaching consensus

TIPS & COACHING:
LEVERAGING YOUR SAGE TALENT

If you discover you've got the Sage Sweet Spot while reading this chapter, these are ways you can experience the most joy, ease and collaboration and create the best results:

> Practice **listening skills** to empower others' participation—Sages, in their exuberance, can talk over others

- Listen; even if you think you know how to do this, ask people if they feel heard
- Learn to ask open-ended questions that elicit others' participation (e.g., questions that are not yes/no or encourage other simple answers)
- Get training in communications skills to learn to listen and reflect back to people what you hear they are saying and not saying
- Develop ways to notice when you are talking too much and strategies for pausing yourself to give others a chance to speak

> Develop increasing **comfort with pauses and silence**—a Sage's desire to keep things flowing and fun can inadvertently take up all the space, making it more difficult for others to participate

- Practice encouraging other people to share their voices (in addition to you sharing your own)
- You have a great sense of timing and rhythm—it is good to trust it and take action, *and* it is important to notice if you are simply filling space because you are nervous or

uncomfortable

- Explore when it feels natural to jump in and when to wait;
you will likely notice signals in your body about when to
take action; practice developing more subtle awareness of
these messages (e.g., not every signal means to speak)
- Before you go into a meeting or into some other setting
in which you will likely have to be quiet for a while, do
something to fully express yourself, such as having a lively
conversation with someone else who also enjoys this

> Plan daily time for **conversations and group interactions**—
Sages are fueled by group experiences

- Plan meetings and conversations throughout your day,
possibly off-site in a fun environment with more people
- Walk around the office and chat with your people in ways
that also support their work flow
- If there aren't enough ways you can create productive
conversations as part of your workday, ensure you
experience enough fun interactions outside of your job
- Work with your door open or in public places so you hear
the background buzz

> **Express yourself**, optionally with stories and metaphors—
Sages often have a lot to share and do it best interactively

- Choose opportunities to express in verbal *and* in animated,
nonverbal ways (e.g., body language, facial expressions and
using your hands)
- Often you'll notice when something needs to be said in a
group (such as an elephant in the room); trust yourself and

express yourself about this, as you're likely very good at it

- You likely use language and speak about topics that others avoid or believe are not politically correct (e.g., cuss words, crass jokes and innuendos); while this can require some discernment, don't stop just because others get uncomfortable, as this is often a huge service
- If you're not as verbal, writing may be your preference—it is still expression
- Trust that your stories and metaphors help people connect with and integrate new ideas—stories help people ground ideas emotionally, making them more tangible and real (stories aren't just for fun)

> Have **as much fun as possible**, whether you are alone or with people—fun is an essential nutrient for a Sage

- Feed your play appetite while at work—listen to music, have relevant toys in your office, put playful art on the walls, etc.
- Choose a career path involving products, services, communities and activities that enable others to have fun
- Select fun activities that positively impact the business (e.g., that encourage participation, build the team and engage customers)

> Participate in and **build communities**—Sages are natural networkers

- Join, start and help run communities; explore how this can be part of your work (e.g., for others in your line of work and for customers)
- Connect people you know to each other and grow your own

networks; you'll enjoy being a central hub

> **Lead groups** in whatever ways are natural for you—Sages aren't always in the spotlight
  - Many Sages prefer to lead by being part of the group, facilitating interactions from within, while others enjoy being at the front of the room and on stage
  - If you prefer to be on stage, ensure that you know how to share the stage with others too

> Utilize your awareness of **patterns**—Sages see them easily
  - Speak about the patterns you see (in data, people, trends, etc.) and notice ways this can inform strategies and decision-making

TIPS & COACHING: WORKING WITH A SAGE

If you discover you are managing or working with someone who has the Sage Sweet Spot:

> Give them opportunities to **be on teams and in communities** with a productive business focus (customer forums, networking groups)—Sages naturally build groups
  - Give them tasks that utilize their natural ability to engage people; if they don't have enough productive interactions with people, they may engage people in ways that distract from business goals
  - If there aren't enough opportunities on the job, recommend they engage in more social activities outside the workplace

> Allow them to **contribute fun** as a productive part of business: fun energizes and relaxes people, connects teams, increases creativity and ultimately empowers better performance—Sages easily make this happen

- Hear them when they suggest activities that may seem useless at first (e.g., including food at a meeting or having a meeting off-site somewhere fun)—experiment to see how it may be of service
- Fun will likely show up spontaneously as well; they may tell jokes or make funny expressions—they notice if people are being too serious and will do something to lighten things up
- If your Sage does get out of hand, appreciate their intention and redirect them to see how their fun can support the business goals as well

> **Sages love to talk**—give them time and space to do so and encourage them to create opportunities on their own time as well

- Beware of scheduling very short meetings with a Sage; they often need to talk when you first connect with them—plan time to relax and let them chat for a while
- If you manage a Sage that tends to talk for too long, set them up ahead of time with a way you'll signal them to finish up because you are about to redirect the conversation— knowing ahead of time that you will interrupt will make it easier for them
- Suggest that they speak to others who love to talk and "get it out of their system" before a meeting or as a way to kick off their day
- Take care when interrupting them, telling them that they

are too loud or talking too much—this can lead them to feel unappreciated and shut down; appreciate their abilities and help them see the unintended impact:

» If they talk for too long at one time, ask them to summarize their ideas in one sentence and move on (and create a method to signal them)

» If they are too loud or crude and others consider them obnoxious, request that they tone it down and close a door or move into a room that is more inviting of this behavior

» Suggest they engage their skills in productive areas of the business: writing, marketing, sales and internal communications

> Encourage them to **include others in communication**—have them focus on creating a conversational flow that weaves a group together

- Encourage them to ask questions of others to invite their participation

- Suggest they get training in and practice learning to listen and reflect back to people what they hear they are saying and not saying

- Recommend they pass around an object (e.g., a talking stick) as people talk, so that the Sage notices how long they are speaking and to encourage them to take turns with others

- Encourage them to explore when it feels natural to jump in and when to wait; Sages tend to notice signals in their bodies about when to take action, and this will help them develop more subtle awareness of these messages (i.e., not every signal means to talk)

> Notice and utilize their ability to **see patterns**—these might be about the business, people, etc.

- Sages are likely to recognize and voice group needs before anyone else has spoken of them
- Appreciate the Sage when they call out the elephant in the room that's not getting addressed, even if this is awkward

> Encourage Sages to **lead in ways that are natural** for them— sometimes as part of the group rather than at the front of the room

- Some Sages like to be humorous storytellers in the spotlight, and others prefer to lead more quietly, not from the back but from the center hub of the room, quietly sensing all that is going on
- They might create informal conversations and discussions with people, greasing the wheels and weaving a web before formal meetings occur
- Sages are the glue that holds groups together, often by communicating messages that shape the culture, so ensure they're spreading the messages and building the culture you want them to

FAMOUS SAGES

Allen Funt	Elton John	Mario Cuomo
Bella Abzug	Fats Domino	Orson Welles
Bette Midler	Franklin D. Roosevelt	Queen Latifah
Bill Clinton	Garrison Keillor	Randolph Hearst
Bob Dole	Gary Zukav	Raquel Welch
Dan Aykroyd	George Bush Sr.	Roseanne Barr
Danny Kaye	George W. Bush Jr.	Sean Connery
David McCallum	Geraldo Rivera	Steve Martin
Dolly Parton	Jay Leno	Steve Wozniak
Don Johnson	John F. Kennedy	Surya Das
Dudley Moore	John McCain	Walter Cronkite
Ed Bradley	Johnny Carson	Wayne Dyer
Eleanor Roosevelt	Lech Wałęsa	Will Rogers
Ellen DeGeneres	Lucille Ball	William Shatner

CHAPTER 4

THE WARRIOR

MARIA, DIRECTOR OF OPERATIONS

Day of GlobalApp's corporate retreat:

I'm staring at the chair I will have to sit in for the next two hours and dreading it. I really detest these kinds of meetings. It's hard for me to sit still that long, but mostly, I don't like wasting time. I do think the leaders here can get things done; it's just that so much of the time is not well used.

At breakfast this morning, Chris asked me how I felt about losing this key client. "It's a tough break," I said, "but I'm not deterred by losing a battle. I'm sure there will be many more—win some and lose some. Let's just keep our future losses to a minimum." I think he was a little taken aback by my lack of a "caring" response, but I don't find mushy conversation productive.

People have started talking, and the first thing I notice is that no one is talking about actions. "People," I say, "we need to be able to assign actions to these ideas. Someone should be taking notes so that when the time for assigning action comes, we don't have to slow down the process and recreate what's been said. Also, we need to determine how to hold each other to account for what we've agreed to do." I think people have gotten by now that repeated, impractical and unfocused work drives me up the wall. Rachel offers to take notes, and I can settle down a little here.

After several of the leaders have gone on, a little too much in my opinion, with tangents or anecdotes, I now have to speak. Brian asks me what I think is the biggest problem GlobalApp has to solve. "Inefficiency," I say. "From the moment I walked in the door, I could see it everywhere—redundant or missed billing, overlap of duties, misplaced reports, messy communication, mismanagement of resources, dysfunctional project managers, lax salespeople with no accountability—the list goes on. Not only that, we waste way too many resources trying to make things look 'cool' and 'unique' while we lose a key client because our processes failed."

I know that last point will make Brian cringe. He's one of those "creative" types whose feathers get ruffled whenever I bring up the idea of structure or rules. But I'm holding my position here—it doesn't matter how brilliant our products are if we can't get them out on time and follow up with clients in a systematic way. I just wish people could get this versus seeing me as some sort of inflexible army sergeant.

What contribution is Maria making, and what unique value does she bring?

What is Maria overly focused on or attached to that is causing frustration?

THE WARRIOR'S CONTRIBUTIONS

Warriors are typically all about action, being effective and producing value. They are often the people behind the scenes who make everything happen as smoothly and efficiently as possible. These are the people you can rely on, who will do what they promised no matter what, and who will move steadily forward toward worthy goals with courage and determination, even in the face of formidable challenges. Warriors are usually extremely grounded, allowing others to feel safe and secure in their solid, stable presence.

In their quest to produce results, Warriors are often masters at **efficiency**. They can have an enhanced awareness of how to **simplify** and streamline processes and systems. They are able to identify waste in any form—time, resources, money or effort—and minimize or eliminate it. American industrialist Andrew Carnegie was said to be possessed by the need to create ever-greater efficiencies—and it made him a fortune. His steel mills boasted the latest equipment in the world, which made the manufacturing of steel incredibly cheap. Whenever newer, more efficient technology appeared, Carnegie ripped out old equipment and replaced it with new equipment to further reduce labor costs and increase production. As a result, his mills always remained the most productive and profitable in the world.

As head of his own production company, Clint Eastwood, American actor turned film director, is also known for his efficiency. He has earned a reputation for filming with a speed and economy that is unusual in the industry. Of the more than 50 films his production company, Malpaso, has made since 1968, it is said that not one finished behind schedule or over budget. "I've just seen a lot of waste in this business," Eastwood says, "a waste of money, of time, of good talent, even. I just thought with Malpaso there could be some kind of alternative there." One of the "alternatives" he introduced was streamlining the process of a production day by negotiating with unions for a ten-hour day in which food would be constantly provided for crew and cast. "That way," Eastwood commented, "you never stop for an official meal break and have the usual inertia that follows afterwards."

Warriors are also known for being both **tactical** and **strategic**, able to see clearly how all pieces of a project fit to achieve their goals and fulfill their ultimate purpose. They are typically **decisive**, and their ability to think abstractly and practically allows them to plot the best course to get them to their destination with certainty. Although there are countless examples of this tactical and strategic quality in the military, Warriors have brought these talents to a variety of other causes and industries as well.

Warrior Booker T. Washington, African American educator, author and orator who became world famous in the late 19th and early 20th centuries, was committed to attaining civil rights for all African Americans. But in 1895, he did not believe that it was the right time strategically to challenge Jim Crow segregation and the disfranchisement of black voters in the South. His tactic was for African Americans to "concentrate all their energies on industrial education, and accumulation of wealth, and the conciliation of the South" with the faith that "blacks would eventually gain full participation in society by showing themselves to be responsible, reliable American citizens." His plan included educating a new generation of African American teachers, building 5,000 schools in the rural South (funded by prominent Warrior Andrew Carnegie and fellow strategist John D. Rockefeller) and promoting a "self-pride" and "self-help" philosophy within the African American community. This strategy eventually led to the financial power, legal education and political support to create the civil rights movement of the 1960s and the passage of important federal civil rights laws. Booker T. Washington saw that the most effective long-term plan would be to build a stronger foundation, empower a broader population of people and yield a larger win over time.

Kirk Douglas, the legendary Hollywood actor, began his career in the mid-1940s under the strong studio system that ran Hollywood and everyone in it. After he achieved critical acclaim playing a selfish boxer in the film *Champion*, Douglas realized that to succeed as a star, he needed to be more strategic about his career and choose tougher, "son of a bitch" roles, as he called them, that would ramp up his intensity. But he also recognized that he would never be given the opportunity to play the parts he sought by staying shackled within the studio system. With a keen eye on long-term strategy, Douglas's tactic was to break his studio contracts and form his own movie company to gain total control over his career and his projects—a move that was completely unheard of in that era. Of that move, he said, "I never thought of being a producer, but I was frustrated because there were certain movies that I wanted to make. So, I formed my company."

Warriors can be highly **effective** at **producing results**. Through massive **action**, by their own hands-on efforts or by skillful use of resources around them, they know how to create **momentum** and stay on point to achieve their goals. Practical and resourceful with excellent follow-through, Warriors generally accomplish whatever they have committed to do.

I've always made a total effort, even when the odds seemed entirely against me. I never quit trying; I never felt that I didn't have a chance to win.
Arnold Palmer

Warrior Harriet Tubman was an African American abolitionist during the American Civil War. She produced astounding results under formidable circumstances. Born into slavery, Tubman escaped and then immediately took action to rescue her family. She brought her relatives out of Maryland, one group at a time, using the network of antislavery activists and safe houses known as the Underground Railroad. On one trip, her husband refused to leave the state. Letting no action go to waste, she found other slaves to take his place and took them to freedom instead. (Note: her husband had already remarried at this time.) Tubman made more than 19 missions to rescue more than 300 slaves. Years later, she told an audience, "I was conductor of the Underground Railroad for eight years, and I can say what most conductors can't say—I never ran my train off the track and I never lost a passenger."

> Some of us have great runways already built for us. If you have one, take off. But if you don't have one, realize it is your responsibility to grab a shovel and build one for yourself and for those who will follow after you.
>
> *Amelia Earhart*

As commander of the Seventh US Army and later the Third US Army during World War II, Warrior General George Patton insisted that "a good plan violently executed now is better than a perfect plan executed next week." When it came to taking immediate actions to produce an intended result, Patton excelled. When ordered to take battered and demoralized troops into action in ten days' time, Patton immediately implemented sweeping changes: ordering his soldiers to wear clean and pressed uniforms, establishing rigorous schedules and requiring strict adherence to military protocol. His actions didn't stop there; he constantly moved among his troops, talking with men, encouraging them, pushing them hard and rewarding them for accomplishments. To keep them battle-ready, Patton took special care of the soldiers under his command, taking the steps necessary to ensure they received extra blankets and socks, galoshes and other items normally in short supply at the front. Once action was put in motion, Patton also understood the importance and efficiency of keeping up the momentum. When asked whether the US Third Army's rapid offensive across France should be slowed to reduce the number of US casualties, Patton replied, "Whenever you slow anything down, you waste human lives."

> The most difficult thing is the decision to act, the rest is merely tenacity. The fears are paper tigers. You can do anything you decide to do. You can act to change and control your life; and the procedure, the process is its own reward.
>
> *Amelia Earhart*

In pursuit of their goals, Warriors are known for their unwavering **persistence** and **perseverance**. In general, Warriors will not give up, maintaining a purposeful focus no matter what they face, and they can show admirable **courage** in facing obstacles and challenges that might dissuade others.

> In order to achieve anything you must be brave enough to fail.
>
> *Kirk Douglas*

Warrior Amelia Earhart was a pioneer in American aviation and the first female pilot to fly solo across the Atlantic Ocean. As a

21-year-old in 1918, Earhart was determined to learn to fly and persevered through both financial and logistical obstacles. She worked at a variety of jobs, including as a photographer, truck driver and stenographer to earn the $1,000 she needed for flying lessons. To reach the airfield, Earhart had to take a bus to the end of the line, and then walk four miles. She was equally persistent in her quest to become a world-renowned aviator. Earhart did whatever it took to raise the money for her record-breaking flights, including writing books, promoting products and speaking across the country to attract sponsors. In 1932, Earhart flew across the Atlantic, becoming the first woman and the second person to do so. In 1935, she was the first pilot to solo across the Pacific and to solo nonstop from Los Angeles to Mexico.

> I don't run away from a challenge because I am afraid. Instead, I run toward it because the only way to escape fear is to trample it beneath your feet.
> *Nadia Comăneci*

Benazir Bhutto, Pakistani prime minister and stateswoman, exemplified a Warrior's courage and persistence throughout her career. As a student at Oxford in the '70s, she persevered in contesting the election in the prestigious debating society to become its first Asian female president. In 1984, after six years of house arrests and brutal imprisonment by Pakistan's military dictatorship, Bhutto and her family were allowed to leave the country for medical reasons. Unwilling to be stopped, she immediately resumed her political activities and raised awareness about the mistreatment of political prisoners by the Pakistani regime. As prime minister, Bhutto never stopped fighting for reforms that threatened the conservative status quo, leading to an attempted coup d'état and later unfounded accusations of corruption that led to her dismissal and self-imposed exile. Still undeterred, after being exonerated on the corruption charges, Bhutto returned to Pakistan and straight back to the political arena—and was assassinated. Death was the only thing that could stop Bhutto's indomitable perseverance.

> Ultimately, leadership is about the strength of one's convictions, the ability to endure the punches, and the energy to promote an idea. And I have found that those who do achieve peace never acquiesce to obstacles, especially those constructed of bigotry, intolerance, and inflexible tradition.
>
> *Benazir Bhutto*

THE WARRIOR UNDERBELLY

Warriors are not always easy people to be around. In their determination to accomplish what they set out to do, Warriors can be exceedingly pushy, often using **intimidation and force**. Harriet Tubman told of being in a group of fugitive slaves where morale was low. When one man decided to head back to his plantation, she pointed a gun at his head saying, "You go on or die." They can be overly aggressive. Dictators like Benito Mussolini used intimidation and force with their "you're either with me or against me" mentality.

Patton was known to use force in dealing with subordinates, at times striking them physically. During the Sicily campaign, controversy ensued when it was said that Patton slapped and verbally abused two soldiers at an evacuation hospital. They were said to be suffering from "battle fatigue," and he ordered them back to the front. Patton also issued orders to his commanders to discipline soldiers with similar claims. Hailed as an effective, aggressive leader by his superiors, Patton's use of force was not viewed as being sufficient for repercussions. Seemingly, his value as a Warrior in battle overshadowed any possible action to curb his use of intimidation and force.

Nobody ever defended anything successfully, there is only attack and attack and attack some more.

George S. Patton

Warriors may not value those around them except as resources. They can have a tendency to **use people as pawns** to attain their goals. Known for his enthusiasm for entering into battle, General Patton was nicknamed Old Blood and Guts, which, as one of his soldiers put it, meant "our blood and his guts." In Andrew Carnegie's quest to make his factories extremely efficient, he clearly made the safety of his workers an afterthought. In these dangerous industrial environments, "protective gear" meant two layers of woolen long johns. Horrible injuries and even deaths were not uncommon.

Once they have determined a course of action, it's nearly impossible to get Warriors to change course. They can be **stubborn** and **inflexible** regarding process and procedure, narrow-mindedly clinging to tried and true methodologies. They might break rules or break rank for efficiency, but they don't extend that same freedom to others.

Warriors can have a **hard time relaxing** and sitting still, and they have a tendency to be **tense**. Clint Eastwood is often described as an **impatient** man, easily bored on a set and constantly working. In an interview about Eastwood, Warner Brothers executive Terry Semel said, "Most major directors or actors will take a hiatus after a film of maybe six months or a year, sometimes longer. But Clint likes to keep working and doing it in these various functions, as actor, director, producer or a combination of these functions." Often, Warriors keep **busy simply to be busy** and can work themselves into the ground.

> I tried being reasonable. I didn't like it.
> *Clint Eastwood*

Because Warriors are so tuned in to efficiency and effectiveness, they can have **trouble trusting** others to get the job done and get it done right. As a result, they tend to **micromanage** or take over and do things themselves that others could handle. They can be so certain that their own process is superior that they won't listen to others' ideas. With a strong tendency to micromanage, Winston Churchill's relationships with his subordinates were often tenuous, especially if it was a good general or admiral who was highly accomplished and clearly effective at their job. He was the type of leader who would constantly walk around, attend just about every meeting and question people at their tasks relentlessly. He believed in hands-on involvement in the details of just about every facet of his team's work. His motto of successful management was to "continue to pester, nag and bite!" He was the ultimate "henpecker" when it came to getting people into action. "I am certainly not one of those who need to be prodded," said Churchill. "In fact, if anything, I am the prod."

OTHER WARRIOR CHARACTERISTICS

Warriors are known to particularly value **hard work** and **accomplishment**. In his first years as president of Tuskegee Institute, Booker T. Washington purchased a former plantation as the permanent site of the campus. Under his direction, he and his students literally built their own school—making bricks; constructing classrooms, barns and outbuildings; and growing their own crops and raising livestock. Warriors also tend to be **hands-on**, personally and physically involved in their project. General Patton went so far as to personally back armored tanks off their transport trains and often rode on top of these tanks when going into battle.

Warriors tend to respect and admire accomplishments over

words. When Douglas MacArthur and George Patton met on the battlefield at Saint-Mihiel, France, the two men did not move until they were done with their conversation while the troops hid from the bombing. In a letter to his wife, Patton said that he actually did want to take cover, but out of respect for MacArthur's accomplishments, he would not budge until MacArthur did. What later ensued was one of the most powerful and effective military partnerships in US history.

....

Hard work has made it easy.
That is my secret. That is why I win.
Nadia Comăneci

....

Preparation and **planning** are key to Warriors' effectiveness. They are generally conscious of possible contingencies and potential roadblocks and deal with them proactively. Warriors can be **consistent, methodical** and skilled at putting structures in place and improving existing systems to ensure reliable results.

....

Preparation, I have often said,
is rightly two-thirds of any venture.
Amelia Earhart

....

Though it can be extraordinarily hard to regain a Warrior's trust once it has been broken, Warriors tend to be extremely **loyal**. In 1958, Kirk Douglas broke the notorious Hollywood blacklist by publicly giving screen credit to a blacklisted writer on one of his films whom he had always considered a trusted ally and an excellent writer. Widely condemned at the time, 30 years later Douglas was lauded for this act of courage and loyalty by the American Civil Liberties Union and the Writers Guild of America.

Warriors are often **grounded** with a strong sense of **physicality** and athleticism, even if their careers or lifestyles aren't particularly physical. Pragmatic in their approach, they are perceived as **steady** and **stable**, the rocks that others can rely on. Warriors typically experience the world using an intelligence they have in their bodies. As a result, they are usually acutely aware of the space around them and can be exceptionally smooth and even elegant in their movement, as is visible in the seemingly effortless accomplishments of the many Warriors who end up as world-class athletes.

WARRIOR STAGES OF DEVELOPMENT

STAGE 1: Warriors in Stage 1 fight against *everything*. They love to fight just for the sake of fighting and seem to get energy from pushing up against whatever is in their way, whether it's a person, process or a system that appears to be the obstacle. They're like playground bullies—belligerent, abusive and aggressive—as they try to force their ideas or desires on others. These Warriors struggle to impose stringent "hierarchies" or chains of command on situations they find themselves in. Overly competitive, they feel constantly frustrated and angry and often act out physically. This obviously makes Stage 1 Warriors difficult to work with or even be around.

When Warriors at this stage don't approve of something or someone, they rarely come up with positive alternatives but use their great strength to protest forcefully, demeaning their "opponents" with blunt criticisms and harsh judgments. They do not choose their battles wisely and take on battles they simply cannot win. In doing so, they're like pit bulls that latch on and refuse to let go, even though they themselves are wounded or dying. Stubborn and intractable, Stage 1 Warriors tend to be utterly ineffective at producing the results they crave.

Though these Warriors are difficult, it helps to acknowledge their anger and frustration and assist them to find more productive ways to express it. Since they truly care about moving forward and producing results, they will benefit by having everything asked of them put in the context of how the action will support getting the result. Ask them what they have an underlying desire to accomplish, and suggest that not fighting people will actually get them where they want to go faster and more efficiently. Have them consider that the energy currently spent fighting others is being wasted and is counterproductive.

STAGE 2: Warriors at this stage are focused on efficiency and results. Though they have become less hostile overall and are better at choosing appropriate battles, they are still intensely impatient and critical of others' efforts and tend to bulldoze other people to accomplish what they want. Stage 2 Warriors are quite competitive and basically feel that they can do everything better and more efficiently than others. They tend to take on too much and avoid delegating, which keeps them extremely busy at the micro level. In their constant busyness and inability to sit still, they tend to miss the broader macro perspective.

Warriors in this stage are concerned about consistency and predictability, so they emphasize hierarchy and structure in all they do. They can be obsessively loyal to "tried and true" systems and become upset if others try to introduce new methods or if they don't follow prescribed rules and regulations. Warriors in Stage 2 are still stubborn and persevere in pursuing their results, but they can be halted and can shift directions, albeit quite reluctantly. Because these Warriors love simplicity and planning ahead, they avoid anything "messy" such as emotions or personal interactions, preferring process over people. They also judge themselves harshly if they neglect to foresee obstacles that appear.

Stage 2 Warriors can be encouraged to become more strategic before jumping in and to operate with the broader picture in mind, rather than constantly busying themselves with detailed tactics in the weeds. It will also help them grow to recognize that they can be even more efficient and effective by working with and through other people to achieve results.

STAGE 3: In this stage, Warriors have shifted from their emphasis on hands-on doing to incorporating abstract thinking as well. They can move between the micro and macro perspectives—the forest and the trees—much more easily, so they're able to incorporate more aspects of any project or problem in their strategies. Stage 3 Warriors are focused on momentum, focusing their efforts effectively rather than merely staying busy, as they act with a clear purpose toward clear and realistic goals.

Interestingly, at this stage, Warriors are not as easily drawn into a fight or battle. They have come to recognize struggle as a sign that there may be a more efficient and effective path to their goals. They have a greater ability to accept change and innovation. They are more willing to include others to get results, but they are still very impatient with others' learning processes, and they reject those whose standards are not similarly high. In this stage, delegating still does not come easily.

Warriors in this stage of constant motion or "doing" would find great benefit in learning to be *still*, allowing the easiest solutions to appear. They also can be encouraged to become better delegators—to trust others to implement portions of the work so that their own efforts can be leveraged and to move from micromanaging to coaching.

STAGE 4: Having learned to delegate, these Warriors have become highly effective. They are able to successfully and smoothly produce results. They are able to remain calm, even in the face of unexpected challenges or obstacles. Stage 4 Warriors value the people around them. They are now aware of others' emotions, and they honor them. Now comfortable with teamwork, they have learned to balance their Warrior directness with tact and to coordinate the flow of people working together. These Warriors have also learned to be more flexible and are able to redirect their efforts and modify their plans without experiencing or creating upset as new priorities or opportunities appear.

WARRIOR SWEET SPOT—KEY POINTS

CORE VALUES & BEHAVIORS

- effective action, productivity, multitasking, momentum
- efficiency, simplicity, being methodical, following a process
- planning, preparation, proactivity
- strategy, tactics, decisiveness
- being hands-on, hard work, accomplishment, perseverance
- abstract thinking
- loyalty, stability, consistency, groundedness

TRIGGERS

- waste, excess
- lack of or poor planning
- resistance

CHALLENGES

- pushy, forceful, intimidating
- stubbornness, inflexibility
- going it alone, not trusting others
- ignoring or undervaluing people, using them as pawns
- tense, impatient, not able to relax, being busy just to stay busy

GREAT ORGANIZATIONAL ROLES

- strategy
- operations, logistics, manufacturing
- process development and improvement
- enforcement
- labor, assembly lines and other work with physical activity

THE WARRIOR LEADER

- makes decisions and implements—strategic and timely
- creates organizational structure—simple and efficient
- puts processes in place and ensures they're followed
- promotes a competitive and driven culture

TIPS & COACHING:
LEVERAGING YOUR WARRIOR TALENT

If you discover you've got the Warrior Sweet Spot while reading this chapter, these are ways you can experience the most joy, ease and collaboration and create the best results:

> Choose projects where you can **take action now**—Warriors need to experience things as moving forward

- Ensure, at least in some of your work, that you can take steps using your own timing and process, with nothing in the way
- Put yourself on projects and teams where you can recommend simple, grounded steps for moving initiatives forward
- When not able to take physical action, such as in meetings with long discussions, find ways you can multitask while still paying attention (while it is becoming a common cultural myth that no one can multitask, Warriors are great at it and energized by it as long as they don't do it to avoid speaking up about something)

> Regularly stop and **step back to look at the bigger picture** to ensure specific actions being done are the most effective at accomplishing the larger purpose

- Broaden your focus to look at integrated strategies in addition to individual tactics
- Check to ensure you're not missing the forest for the trees—pause, look up, take a breath, recall the larger purpose and see if a different action would be a more efficient way to achieve it
- Look for opportunities to shift from planning concrete and practical steps to thinking more abstractly about the entire work-flow process—Warriors have an innate sense of how individual efforts can integrate together to optimize an entire system

> **Choose the easy solution rather than hard work** in order to be more productive—Warriors have so much strength and perseverance that they can confuse being forceful with being truly effective

- Notice where you are doing work for the sake of doing work, and see how you can direct this energy into something that yields a more valuable result
- Shift the context of how you determine value—give yourself and others credit for accomplishments that don't require a lot of effort and hard work

> Learn to **stretch into new and unknown** territory as well as being comfortable doing what is already familiar—Warriors often default to what they already know works

- Before making decisions based on previous experience, consider what untried methods might be more efficient and effective
- When other people suggest new ideas, create methods that enable you to pause and breathe before immediately saying, "No!"
- When a team that you are part of chooses to explore a new and hopefully better process, instead of resisting this, put your energy into determining how this new way can save time, money and other resources

> Achieving results in business requires working with other people, so it is essential to be able to recognize and **work with their feelings and emotions** and the impact you have on them—Warriors often think or wish feelings were irrelevant, and they're not

- Calm yourself down before giving feedback to others and express your feelings before your frustration builds up; if you don't, your approach may be too intense for others, and they'll miss the value of your recommendations
- When you have feedback to share, use language that addresses the process, not the person, because others may experience your intensity as aggression—also, take care about where and how you direct your gaze so others don't experience you as forceful (i.e., don't stare people down)
- To navigate the feelings and emotions of others, it will be necessary to recognize your own feelings too, ideally by recognizing how you experience feelings in your body

> Include and **collaborate with other people** to expand capacity and increase overall effectiveness—Warriors can limit results by insisting on doing too much themselves

- Genuinely explore how it could be more efficient to utilize other people
- Clarify when it is really necessary to do something "your way" and when allowing others to do something "their way" enables them to be more cooperative and ultimately more productive—remember that even though you might do the same task more quickly, you likely provide more value by doing something else instead
- Business requires working with other people, so to grow in your career, you'll need to figure this out—consider it a strategic game to make collaboration work

> **Get up and move** if you sit a lot—Warriors need enough movement and action happening so they flow well

- Take a break from intellectual work to get up and move your body, particularly if you get impatient with structures and processes that seem constraining (such as during a long meeting or long task on a computer)
- Consider using a standing desk or sitting on a moving chair or exercise ball

> **Take time to stop moving and clear your mind**—Warriors tend to densely compact activities, but they increase their capacity with ease and collaboration when they experience more space

- Take a break to do a slow, methodical walking meditation in the middle of the day

- Enjoy simple, repetitive tasks as they fit naturally in your work flow, as they're likely clearing and relaxing—this can even be cleaning out emails, walking around the office, following a regular process for preparing for meetings, etc.

TIPS & COACHING: WORKING WITH A WARRIOR

If you discover you are managing or working with someone who has the Warrior Sweet Spot:

> **Discuss strategies** with them—they are naturally good at this and will be more motivated
- Include them when designing strategies, as the results will be better, and they'll also be more likely to do tasks and follow requests that support implementation
- Share higher-level strategies that are handed down as much as you can—they'll relax knowing how their work fits in with the larger plan
- Be willing to hear them out when they disagree and see what, if any, improvements can be made; this prevents them from fighting against what's happening
- If a less mature or tired Warrior gets lost in the tactics, remind them to come back up to the bigger strategy

> Encourage them to **include others** in decision-making and implementation—Warriors have a tendency to do too much themselves
- Remind them that controlling, micromanaging and doing

everything on their own decreases their effectiveness and capacity

- Support them to take small steps with delegation and cooperation
- Encourage them to recognize how others' contributions can increase capacity and results over time—and they may need help to see how other people's ways of doing things can be equally or sometimes even more effective

> Help them to understand how their poor "bedside manner" can decrease efficiency—encourage them to consider their **impact on people**

- Warriors must learn and accept that people with many different Talents are often needed for efficient implementation, so it is essential to include and honor a variety of people (specifically those who are not Warriors)
- Help them learn that it is not just the content but also the context of how they communicate that impacts people (frustrated Warriors can inadvertently be passive aggressive)—little things like their attitude, movements, expressions, etc., make a big difference
- Hear their frustration about working with people and help them devise ways to be more patient and curious when working with others (e.g., do solitary activities that they are highly efficient at before meetings, plan ways to multitask or take breaks during longer interactions)
- Support them to see how holding grudges only holds them back—help them to see what actions they can take now to help things move forward smoothly in the future and to let

go of the past

> Encourage them to explore and discover the **utility of feelings and emotions**—this is often a huge step for Warriors
  - Encourage them by demonstrating how emotions can be used strategically to move an agenda forward
  - Encourage them to celebrate and see that celebration increases capacity and results
  - Support them to understand and forgive themselves for their own fits of frustration while simultaneously learning to express anger in healthy ways, directly and promptly, instead of passive aggressively
  - Help them become aware of how emotions control them if they don't know how to work with emotions

> Encourage them to **trust their capacity in the unknown**—they are good at navigating new territory but often prefer to do what is familiar
  - Warriors are not likely to admit they feel scared, and proposals for doing things in new ways are likely to bring up their concerns that they (and the others they feel responsible for) might not accomplish all they set out to do—help them see how they can feel more at ease in the unknown so that they can engage new strategies and tactics that can improve effectiveness
  - Remind them that they'll excel and be more competitive when they can incorporate new ways

> Support them to see how they can **allow everything to be easier**—Warriors often think they don't provide value unless they

do hard work

- Ask them, "How could this be easier for you and the team?" and, if needed, ask, "Are you willing to allow this to happen more easily?"
- Warriors will often try to "hold" or be responsible for more than is theirs because they worry about the efficiency and effectiveness of the whole, so hear their concerns, see if there is an appropriate way for them to offer their feedback to others and refocus them on their own domain

FAMOUS WARRIORS

Amelia Earhart	Clint Eastwood	Mr. T
Andre Agassi	Corazon Aquino	Nadia Comăneci
Andrew Carnegie	Danica Patrick	Rosie O'Donnell
Arnold Palmer	David Hasselhoff	Ruth Bader Ginsburg
Benazir Bhutto	Diego Maradona	Serena Williams
Benito Mussolini	George Patton	Tina Turner
Carl Lewis	John Wayne	
Charles Bronson	Malcolm X	

CHAPTER 5

THE SERVER

RACHEL, DIRECTOR OF HUMAN RESOURCES

Day of GlobalApp's corporate retreat:

It's 8:55 a.m. The meeting is about to begin, and Kevin is not here yet. Is he okay? Did he get the right directions? I'm hoping that Brian is going to use some sort of format for the meeting that will ensure everyone gets heard and that the others are actually listening. The last meeting was basically a platform for a few people to state their opinions while the rest of us were left in the dust.

From the start, I have always loved this company's values, but it's things like the meeting format and making sure people have the right directions that keep bothering me. I know our leadership team cares about their people, yet, somehow, people's needs are being overlooked. This is what has been so upsetting for me about losing a key client like we did. I feel awful that somehow their needs were simply not being met, and no one noticed, not even me.

Maria is now responding to Brian's question in the meeting about what GlobalApp's biggest problem is. She is making points about efficiency and processes, and my heart is sinking. I feel like it is this very lack of focus on the human side of our business that has impacted both our employees and our clients, and it's hurting our revenue and retention. I am definitely going to speak up about this, but I will wait until it's my turn. I see no reason to be rude and interrupt Maria.

Finally, it's my turn to answer Brian's question. "In my view," I say, "our biggest problem is that our clients and employees aren't being honored and appreciated. We are focusing too much on what's wrong with the processes, logistics, budgets, technology, etc., when what we really need to do is listen. If someone had listened more closely to our key client, we would never have lost them. Also, our employees don't feel sufficiently valued, so they are not going that extra, yet essential, mile. With better performance management, better training and clearer feedback, our people would be much more equipped to listen and meet our client's needs and feel that their own needs are being met as well."

I'm not certain if what I just said really sank in. Honestly, I don't like talking in front of everybody. I worry that I will make someone feel uncomfortable or make them look bad in front of everyone else, but I really feel strongly that if I don't keep speaking up, nothing will change.

> What contribution is Rachel making, and what unique value does she bring?
>
> What is Rachel overly focused on or attached to that is causing frustration?

THE SERVER'S CONTRIBUTIONS

In everyone's life, at some time, our inner fire goes out. It is then burst into flame by an encounter with another human being. We should all be thankful for those people who rekindle the inner spirit.

Albert Schweitzer

The most common major theme for Servers is **love**. They tend to have big hearts that, though easily wounded, offer compassion, genuine caring and a desire to ease the suffering of all living things. Servers are able to connect with others and have an acute intelligence when it comes to interpersonal relationships. They often wear their hearts on their sleeves and can be extremely tender and sensitive. At the same time, they can be ferociously protective when they sense others are being harmed or dishonored. Healers, volunteers, supporters and protectors—Servers are likely to accept and love us just as we are, showing us how to accept and love ourselves.

With their **big hearts**, Servers are often empathetic and sensitive. They tend to **feel others' pain acutely** and are not shy about offering their compassion when other people might turn away. Princess Diana exemplified this quality often in her hands-on charitable work. In 1987, she was photographed while she sat on the sick bed of a man with AIDS, holding his hand. Empathizing with the victim's pain at a time when many people were still afraid that AIDS might be contracted through casual contact, her sensitivity proved bigger than her fear. This simple act of the heart helped change public opinion, showing the world that people with AIDS didn't deserve rejection or isolation but instead deserved compassion and kindness.

Servers have a tendency to **see love everywhere**, in everyone and everything. They can be disturbed by unkindness and seek to expand love wherever they go. Classic Server Fred Rogers was the gentle host of the children's television program *Mister Rogers' Neighborhood* for over 30 years. As caring offscreen as he appeared on camera, Rogers said that he began his career in response to what he saw on a television show ("something horrible on it with people throwing pies at one another") geared toward children. "I went into television because I hated it so, and I thought there was some way of using this fabulous instrument to be of nurture to those who would watch and listen."

People are often drawn to Servers, who tend to naturally **accept and appreciate others** for who they are. Friends of Fred Rogers said that early in his life, he had decided that he would never focus on the outsides of people, but he would look below the surface to see what was essential and good about them. Princess Diana embodied this type of acceptance and appreciation of others. A friend said of her, "She had the gift of making other people feel very good." In the last interview before her death, Princess Diana acknowledged, "I am much closer to people at the bottom than to people at the top." Servers usually want to meet and love human beings simply as they are and appreciate and care for them—to show them they matter.

> Never lose sight of the fact that the most important yardstick of your success will be how you treat other people—your family, friends, and coworkers, and even strangers you meet along the way.
> *Barbara Bush*

Servers typically **honor all people** and believe in human dignity and the sanctity of life. The organization that Cesar Chavez, cofounder of the national United Farm Workers Association (UFW), inspired was not intended to be a labor union. He was not only concerned with wages and working conditions of the laborers but also determined to reclaim honor for people who had been marginalized by society. What started as the Delano Grape Strike came to be known as la Causa (the Cause). Throughout his life, Chavez fought for people who were consistently dishonored and mistreated. Former president Clinton said that "the farm workers who labored in the fields and yearned for respect and self-sufficiency pinned their hopes on this remarkable man." Cesar Chavez's deep commitment to honoring people knew no bounds. Not only did he fight for the dignity of individuals but also for the honoring of all cultures, not just his own. "Preservation of one's own culture," said Chavez, "does not require contempt or disrespect for other cultures."

> How sad it is that we give up on
> people who are just like us.
> *Fred Rogers*

Servers are likely to assume that others have the best intentions, even if they have opposing views. They can be **quick to forgive** and slow to judge others harshly. They usually assume people are doing the best they can and easily move past mistakes or injuries in order to move forward together. Even in dire circumstances, Martin Luther King Jr. expressed this profound forgiveness. As a young preacher in 1956, he came home to find that his home had been bombed and that a long-angry crowd had gathered with chains and weapons to retaliate against the white community. But King would not allow them to do so. Over the next several years, he built an entire movement based on responding to violence and hate with nonviolent resistance and forgiveness.

Nelson Mandela was another Server who showed an amazing capacity to forgive. Imprisoned for 27 years, he would not allow himself to become consumed by bitterness. While Mandela was in prison, the man who was the architect of apartheid, Hendrik Verwoerd, died. As soon as Mandela was released, he visited Verwoerd's widow to express his condolences. "The first lesson is forgiveness," Mandela said in an interview. "You must not allow hate to fester in your brain. You can never allow racism, hatred, and bitterness to rent space in your head." By being magnanimous to his former enemies, Mandela set an example and set his entire country on a path of reconciliation.

> We must develop and maintain the capacity to forgive. He who is devoid of the power to forgive is devoid of the power to love. There is some good in the worst of us and some evil in the best of us. When we discover this, we are less prone to hate our enemies.
> *Martin Luther King Jr.*

Though they are loving and forgiving, Servers can also be ferociously **protective** and **courageous** in fighting for the underdog. They take strong stands, supporting causes that protect people, animals and the earth. Knowing that it would eventually take his life, Martin Luther King Jr. displayed unyielding courage during the civil rights movement. Decades later, his fierce stand for nonviolence in the face of brutal and eventually fatal treatment still remains one of the most inspiring acts of courage worldwide.

As a well-developed Server, MLK's unshakeable conviction that all God's people deserved to be protected under just laws gave him the strength to break laws he felt were unjust despite overwhelmingly abusive and violent reactions. Beyond civil rights, King advocated for many others he felt needed to be protected, even though his life was constantly being threatened by those who opposed his agenda. He spoke out against the war in Vietnam, supported laborers who were striking for better working conditions and demanded that the federal government take action against unemployment and poverty across the country. For Servers, it can be difficult, if not impossible, to turn away from someone who needs help.

> Nothing brings me more happiness than trying to help the most vulnerable people in society. It is a goal and an essential part of my life—a kind of destiny. Whoever is in distress can call on me. I will come running wherever they are.
> *Princess Diana*

Mother Teresa, a deeply committed Server, displayed enormous courage in risking her own life in her quest to protect those she described as "the hungry, the naked, the homeless, the crippled, the blind, the lepers, all those people who feel unwanted, unloved, uncared for throughout society, people that have become a burden to the society and are shunned by everyone." As a young nun in 1948, she left the safe confines of her convent to live alone among the impoverished people of Calcutta. Homeless and with no income, she resorted to begging for food and supplies in order to protect the people. In 1982, at the height of the Siege of Beirut, Mother Teresa brokered a temporary cease-fire to rescue 37 children trapped in a frontline hospital. Though her diaries reveal that she experienced doubt and severe loneliness, Mother Teresa remained determined to care for and protect "the poorest of the poor," putting her own life at risk several times over.

Servers will often go out of their way to **make small gestures** to ensure the **people around them feel important and cared for.** Fred Rogers not only reinforced messages of positive self-worth to his young audiences, but he also regularly sent notes of support to his adult friends and acquaintances. Every summer, to show his care for his staff, Rogers rented out a local amusement park for a day for his employees' children. Not only did he go out of his way to show care for his staff, he kept in contact with reporters who interviewed him, calling now and then to see how they were doing and to hear about their families.

> You are never strong enough
> that you don't need help.
> *Cesar Chavez*

As president of South Africa, Nelson Mandela promoted legislation to support his people in seemingly small ways that he somehow intuitively sensed would make a big difference. Knowing how important rugby was to the pride of the Afrikaners, Mandela went out of his way to support South Africa's national rugby team, even though this team had been a symbol of racism and Afrikaner power for decades. Though the world had shunned the team during the apartheid years, Mandela helped bring them back into international competition and fulfilled their dream to host the World Cup in South Africa. The seemingly small issue of the rugby team made an enormous impact on national pride.

This gesture also points to a Server's ability to find ways to touch people's lives directly, not in a nebulous, "trickle-down" type of approach.

Servers are generally **able to genuinely connect quickly and fully** with others. They tend to prefer one-on-one interactions and want others to feel fully understood. On his television show, Fred Rogers didn't talk at his preschool audience but conversed with them. He connected with the children on their level and expressed a sincere interest in their lives and challenges. When talking to children individually, Rogers actually crouched down to look them in the eyes. He said, "One of the greatest gifts you can give anybody is the gift of your honest self. I also believe that kids can spot a phony a mile away." He understood that if you want a connection with a kid, you have to be genuine.

....

> Pity may represent little more than the impersonal concern which prompts the mailing of a check, but true sympathy is the personal concern which demands the giving of one's soul.
> *Martin Luther King Jr.*

....

Though a member of the British Royal Family, Princess Diana had the ability to connect effortlessly with everyone, including "commoners." As one of her friends said, "She was a princess but she could step down and make you feel special."

Cesar Chavez, who was bilingual, made sure to speak in English to non-Mexican audiences, reporters and people on college campuses. But he always spoke to his Mexican followers in Spanish, the language that was most comfortable to them, and kept his speeches simple and down-to-earth. He was known for his ability to truly connect with people on their level. He once remarked, "If you really want to make a friend, go to someone's house and eat with him…the people who give you their food give you their heart."

THE SERVER UNDERBELLY

Servers should not be confused with saints. Though basically loving, they can also be **mean** and **lash out** when they are thwarted or when they witness a lack of compassion toward themselves or others. The manifestation of this meanness could range from overall demeanor to small, biting comments. They can be good at "sticking the knife in and twisting it" with precision because they are so attuned to the sensitivities of others.

Nelson Mandela, speaking passionately against a potential war in Iraq, publicly lashed out at both former UK Prime Minister Tony Blair and then-President George W. Bush for what he saw as racism. "Both Bush as well as Tony Blair are undermining an idea that was sponsored by their predecessors. They do not care. Is it because this Secretary General of the United Nations is now a black man?" he said, referring to Kofi Annan. "They never did that when secretary generals were white." As Mandela's presidential predecessor F. W. de Klerk commented, "He was by no means the avuncular, saint-like figure depicted today. As an opponent he could be brutal and quite unfair."

Martin Luther King Jr. similarly lashed out at white Southern churches and their leaders that didn't support the civil rights movement, even questioning the sincerity of their Christian faith by saying, "What kind of people worship here? Who is their God?"

Servers can also become self-appointed **martyrs, using guilt to manipulate** others. When questioned about a sexist remark, Cesar Chavez became enraged and said, "I work eighteen #!&%*ing hours a day for the union. Who of you can say the same?"

> Being unwanted, unloved, uncared for, forgotten by everybody, I think that is a much greater hunger, a much greater poverty than the person who has nothing to eat.
> *Mother Teresa*

Because of their sometimes desperate **craving for love**, Servers can become intensely **needy**, like energy vampires who can never get enough. Princess Diana was so in need of constant love and attention that, according to friends, she called them numerous times each day. Author Penny Junor claimed that Diana "needed constant reassurance, constant attention, constant love" and that Prince Charles made all sorts of attempts to meet her needs, including getting rid of anything she didn't like whether it be staff, friends or even pets, but "nothing seemed to make her happy."

Not finding the deep connection they crave, Servers can feel **very lonely** and may react by **disconnecting** from any real relationships to avoid being hurt. Though from a large family, Ted Kennedy experienced severe loneliness in his childhood, attending ten boarding schools in 11 years and losing three siblings before the age of 16. After the assassination of his brother Robert, Ted Kennedy retreated from the world and spent the next ten weeks brooding and sailing alone off Cape Cod.

Servers tend to be **overly sensitive, taking everything personally**. They show their emotions on the outside and may overreact when others are hurt. When Martin Luther King Jr. was 12, he blamed himself for his grandmother's death, because the younger brother he was supposed to be watching accidentally knocked her unconscious while sliding down a banister. The incident had nothing to do with her subsequent heart attack, but King attempted suicide by jumping from a second-story window. He was distraught for days, unable to sleep, a pattern that was similar to the bouts of depression he suffered during the civil rights movement.

Grief is the price we pay for love.
Queen Elizabeth II

Because of their heart-focused lives, Servers can also experience **intense pain** and **deep sadness**. Mother Teresa expressed this pain and sadness in her early days in Calcutta when she wrote, "There is such terrible darkness within me, as if everything was dead. It has been like this more or less from the time I started 'the work.' In my heart there is no faith—no love—no trust—there is so much pain—the pain of longing, the pain of not being wanted. I want God with all the powers of my soul—and yet there between us—there is terrible separation."

....

> There can be no deep disappointment
> where there is not deep love.
> *Martin Luther King Jr.*

....

In their desire to serve, Servers may become overly **self-sacrificing**, jeopardizing their health and well-being or **working themselves to exhaustion**. Cesar Chavez fasted to promote and publicize nonviolent activism. Taking it to dangerous extremes, he fasted for 24, 25 and even 36 days on water only. Mother Teresa's diaries reveal that she was often emotionally and physically exhausted.

OTHER SERVER CHARACTERISTICS

Servers are often **devoted** friends, **faithful** and **loyal** in all circumstances. They tend to believe in the good intentions of others and **accept** them for who they are, as they are. They are often extraordinarily inclusive, sensitive to anyone being left out or disenfranchised. On the other hand, because of their implicit faith in people, Servers can be **naïve** and **undiscerning**, which allows others to take advantage of them. They have a tendency to **love**

fully, but often pick partners who don't love them in return.

Servers can be amazingly **unselfish** and are often happy to perform in support positions behind the scenes without fanfare or limelight. Servers can be incredibly **patient** and exhibit great endurance in their support of causes or people. They tend to be **humble** and simple in their dress, appearance and speech. Their satisfaction often comes from the sense that they have truly helped others, and though they like to be appreciated, they may be uncomfortable receiving accolades for what they do.

> If I can bring joy into the world, if I can get people to stop thinking about their pain for a moment, or the fact [that] tomorrow morning they're going to get up and tell their boss off...then I'll be successful.
>
> *Bobby McFerrin*

Others can appreciate Servers for being **sincere** and **genuine**. Servers can make themselves fully present to others, offering the gift of their undivided attention and caring. A fully developed Server often exhibits a **sweet playfulness** that invites others to be open and expressive.

However, when Servers aren't able to get the love and connection they want, they can **try too hard** and, uninvited, they attempt to **enmesh themselves** in others' lives. They may become busybodies, offering unsolicited opinions and unwanted assistance and interference. They might feel that they know what support is needed by those around them and seek to make it happen.

Some may see this as an intense need to control all aspects of a situation. In planning an event, Servers may be the ones to take control of everything from the invitation to the food, with little input from others.

SERVER STAGES OF DEVELOPMENT

STAGE 1: Servers in this stage are extremely unhappy and miserable. Their open hearts have become deeply wounded because they have not received enough love and now take almost everything personally. Feeling too vulnerable, they shut down and disconnect from anyone who could possibly hurt them. They will not accept support when it is offered and refuse to offer support to others. Shutting themselves off from people around them, Stage 1 Servers are racked with the pain of terrible loneliness.

These Servers are bitter, feeling that love itself has betrayed them. They blame others for the pain they feel and experience themselves as victims. In turn, the Server reacts by being mean, twisting their intrinsic loving nature into one that is almost hateful. They indiscriminately seek revenge, and, because they are so attuned to the hearts of others, they are particularly good at attacking in ways that hurt the most. In this Stage, Servers can be directly or passively aggressive and incredibly controlling.

To move from this stage, the Server must begin to accept responsibility for their situation and see how they are preventing connection from occurring. If those around them can empower these Servers to acknowledge even tiny connections with others and begin to connect with themselves, they'll start to experience a little bit of the love that they so desperately desire.

STAGE 2: Servers in this stage know they want love, but they can't yet figure out how to get it. They give support in order to be loved, possibly in a needy and/or manipulative manner, but don't feel supported in return. They are now willing to be supportive of others, but they take it to extremes—fearing that the connection they now experience may go away. They can get lost in the care-taking of others—constantly "doing" for others and sacrificing their own needs and desires in the process. They are desperate to feel connection and to experience being loved. However, others perceive this craving as needy and cloying and tend to back away. When these people end up leaving, the Servers often imagine they've been completely taken advantage of. They are left feeling drained; they become martyrs.

To get love and connection, Stage 2 Servers manipulate others to draw them close. Hoping to find more ways in, these Servers may become busybodies, acting with a harsh "tough love," saying they "know what is good for you." They attempt to get others enmeshed to stay in connection. These Servers don't discern who is open to their love and will return it, so they open their hearts to everyone, leaving themselves open to being constantly hurt. Their desperation also attracts people who realize they can take advantage of them and often pushes away the very people and connections that would be good for them.

To grow, Servers in Stage 2 must begin to learn to love and appreciate themselves. It's important that they begin to see that it's okay if they don't connect with everyone and that they are loved not just for what they do but also for who they are. These Servers will need to grapple at this point with how to set better boundaries for themselves. As simple as this sounds, this is incredibly challenging for a Server, almost counterintuitive, but critical to growth at this stage.

STAGE 3: In Stage 3, Servers are beginning to come into their own. They are much more authentically loving of themselves and others, though this love tends to be somewhat conditional. They still thrive on connection with others but are no longer dependent on it for a sense of well-being. They feel compassion and a genuine caring for all living things, and they can be exceedingly patient. Stage 3 Servers are particularly considerate and empathetic and can be fiercely protective when they sense that others are being dishonored or hurt.

Servers in this stage have learned to make better choices for themselves in terms of who they connect with and how they can best support those around them. Though they have learned to say no when it's appropriate, they may still feel guilty about doing so. If they slip into sacrificing themselves at times or taking something too personally, they don't stay caught up in this for long.

Stage 3 Servers will grow by continuing to expand their capacity to abundantly love and care for themselves. They become less serious and invite others to play. As they allow their loving nature to develop, they will begin to love more unconditionally and choose personal and professional partners who will offer this level of genuine connection back to them.

STAGE 4: Servers in this Stage radiate unconditional love, and they express an infinite faith in people. They are empathetic and gracefully forgiving. In their presence, others feel fully accepted and authentically worthy. These Servers exude a sense of peace and serenity, joy and harmony, with an ease that is playful and light. Humble and unassuming, they show others by their own example how to love and accept one another and themselves. They take good care of themselves, and, when they take care of others, it is healthy, natural and balanced.

SERVER SWEET SPOT—KEY POINTS

CORE VALUES & BEHAVIORS
- huge heart—love, compassion, sharing feelings
- connection, intimacy, sincerity
- acceptance, appreciation, honoring others
- care, support, making small gestures to have others feel important
- protection of all living creatures (e.g., people, animals and plants)
- patience, humility, unselfishness

TRIGGERS
- insensitivity—direct or indirect
- meanness
- neglect
- seeing others in pain

CHALLENGES

- too nice to others, naïve
- not honoring, caring for or loving themselves; being self-sacrificing
- taking things personally, lashing out when hurt
- intensity of feelings—pain, loneliness, sadness, desire to disconnect
- needy, cloying martyrdom
- not honoring boundaries, getting into others' business, enmeshment
- manipulation

GREAT ORGANIZATIONAL ROLES

- administration, executive support
- human resources, talent management
- customer service
- caregiving and service industries for people, animals and plants
- healing arts, conventional and alternative medicine practitioners
- nonprofit organizations, volunteering

THE SERVER LEADER

- honors everyone—employees, customers, vendors, etc.
- pursues a larger cause or mission
- has personal, one-on-one interactions
- exhibits fierce protection (healthy or defensive)

TIPS & COACHING:
LEVERAGING YOUR SERVER TALENT

If you discover you've got the Server Sweet Spot while reading this chapter, these are ways you can experience the most joy, ease and collaboration and create the best results:

> Choose opportunities to **care for, honor and express compassion** with colleagues, clients and everyone—Servers need and thrive on this

- Choose to work in organizations that provide products and services that further these values and/or that focus on their culture and invest in their people
- Select roles where your focus is to advocate for others, influence policies honoring people and empower people to take actions to care for themselves
- Create experiences for others to share their feelings and be heard

> Participate in enough **small groups and one-on-one interactions**—Servers thrive on the deeper intimacy that is more frequent in these settings

- When days are filled with many large meetings or a lot of working alone, plan lunches, spontaneous breaks or working meetings with one person at a time
- Integrate remembering meaningful personal details about others in professional ways

> Model **putting on one's own oxygen mask first** before taking care of others—Servers can't sustain their energy and

contributions if they don't do this

- Particularly if you are dedicated and work hard for your organization, it is important that you plan your life with some balance—giving time to yourself and doing activities you love, even if they are just simple things
- Care for, honor and be compassionate with yourself too; learn to let go when feeling guilty for putting yourself first—this is part of the journey

> Sometimes the most caring thing is to **say no to helping others**—Servers walk a fine line between supporting and empowering people vs. disempowering them with caretaking

- While advocating for others, ensure that you don't merely give them food without teaching them to fish—support people to realize themselves what they need and want and coach them on how to make requests
- Ensure that you don't take on too much within your organization—loading your plate with what are really other people's responsibilities can easily turn into more than you can hold, leading you to become a martyr, which undermines both you and the way people relate to you
- Speaking up about what you see isn't being done can be an enormous service in and of itself and is often all that is needed
- Learn to **ask for support** for yourself—Servers often avoid requesting assistance, worrying that others will judge them as needy or that it will be hard on those they are asking (just as it is hard for them if they habitually overcare for others)
- Delegate clearly and completely and make clear agreements

so that you set others up to provide all you want

- Sometimes asking for support includes asking others to be with you while you share your feelings, without them giving you suggestions and advice
- Focus on what's happening now and what steps you and others can take (avoiding complaining about others or the past)

> **Rather than taking things personally** that aren't intended this way, see how you are not honoring yourself about this topic—a Server's sensitivity can lead them to mix up blaming someone for hurting them in the moment vs. feeling sad about not doing something as well as they'd wished, losing an opportunity or feeling pain about something from the past

- Take preventative actions to love, believe in and appreciate yourself on a regular basis, personally and professionally so that you don't have self-doubts that get in the way
- Practice hearing others share about their own experiences and feelings while reminding yourself that they are sharing about themselves—they are not telling you about you (and remember that even if they try to tell you that it is about you that you don't have to believe it)
- Look to see what you've not resolved from the past that is creeping into your present and take steps to let it go

TIPS & COACHING: WORKING WITH A SERVER

If you discover you are managing or working with someone who has the Server Sweet Spot:

> **Interact with them one-on-one** when you can—give them an opportunity to share what they feel about what is happening for them in the workplace

- They may have more to share about their feelings than other employees, and this is beneficial if it doesn't go on too long or turn into complaining
- **Don't multitask** when with them (it is offensive to Servers); schedule a time when you can give them your full attention
- Take care to hear them so they have the experience of being heard—don't jump to giving them advice, and then, if relevant, ask them if there is an action they want to take about the situation

> Give or have them choose **projects and people to support and care for**—this is easy and natural for them

- Ensure that they have enough direct interaction with people—colleagues, clients, etc.
- Encourage them to connect with people at the beginning of and throughout their day

> **Coach them on saying no, giving constructive feedback and facing conflict**—Servers are often too nice and avoid conflict

- Reorient them so that they see that addressing a situation that is not working as well as it ought to be and taking steps to better the situation is actually the most caring thing that can be done

- Servers often struggle with documenting poor performance or firing people because they worry about dishonoring others and hurting them; they need support to realize it is harmful not only to the company and themselves but also to the employee—it is in everyone's best interest to move forward to situations that are a better fit

> Encourage them to **check in with and care for themselves**— Servers can get distracted caring for others, which is not sustainable

- Ask them, "How do you feel?" and "What do you want?"
- Or ask, "What would support you this week, and how can you create that?"

> Encourage them to **directly ask for support and connection** from others—when Servers learn to request and receive support, they'll actually get better at truly caring for (rather than caretaking) others

- Have them look at what they can delegate and agree to take action on
- If they don't see something, have them stretch by asking, "If you could make an unreasonable request of the team/ staff what would that be?" Follow up with, "How could you ask for [some of] that?" and "By when do you think you could make this request?"
- Check to see if there is anything you can do for them

> Help them to **not take things personally**—Servers often have big open hearts that feel hurt more frequently and more easily,

even when no one is targeting them

- If they do take something personally when that's not what was intended, ask, "Would you be willing to consider this had nothing to do with you?"
- If needed, have them separate out what happened (the facts) from the stories they made up about what happened (their interpretation of the facts)
- To refocus them, have them focus on their strengths (mention a few) in ways that are independent of other people's perspectives
- Ask them, "How can you stay focused regardless of how others respond to you?"

> **Appreciate** all they do and their intentions—Servers typically don't ask for recognition, so others need to notice and acknowledge them

- Literally say, "I appreciate that you..."
- Tell them that you noticed how much care and attention they put into a project, an interaction, etc.

FAMOUS SERVERS

Albert Schweitzer

Alice Bailey

Amy Adams

Aung San Suu Kyi

Barbara Bush

Bobby McFerrin

Branford Marsalis

Caesar Chavez

Carl Rogers

Chiang Kai-Shek

Claire Danes

Creed Bratton

Eddie Steeples

Emilio Estevez

Fred Rogers

Gary Cooper

Harry Morgan

Janet Lynn

Jerry Stiller

Leslie David Baker

Louisa May Alcott

Martin Luther King

Melissa McCarthy

Mother Teresa

Phil Donahue

Princess Diana

Queen Elizabeth

Ralph Nader

Roy Rogers

Ted Kennedy

Tyne Daly

CHAPTER 6

THE SCHOLAR

LISA, VICE PRESIDENT OF FINANCE

Day of GlobalApp's corporate retreat:

The meeting is about to start, and I'm definitely prepared. And I bet that no one else is. Losing one of our key clients has me very concerned because I believe that if we don't look closely at the data and track this client's history, we will make the same mistakes and lose more good clients. I'm concerned that if the rest of the leadership can't see my point here, they may make decisions in this meeting based on too little information, or worse, only follow their "gut" about it. It's happened before.

The meeting is in full swing now, and it's Rachel's turn to speak. She talks a lot about people not being heard, not being appreciated, etc. I have to say something after she finishes—I am annoyed. "Help me understand this, Rachel," I blurt out. "I don't deny that appreciation of the client and our staff might be less frequent than it should be and that listening is a key skill, but what information do you have to back this up? How do we know that this is directly or indirectly linked to them leaving?" I want to ask her if she has any, even incidental, feedback that this is linked to why we lost the client or if she has done any staff surveys to give us real data; however, I'm fairly certain she hasn't, and I don't want to upset her and get her all emotional. That has not worked well for me in the past…but sometimes, I just get so tired of the touchy-feely stuff.…

It's now my turn to answer Brian's question. "So, Lisa," Brian says, "what do you think is the biggest problem GlobalApp has?"

I say, "We need to look at trends of current clients so we can take action sooner. One, we could have predicted there was a problem from the increasing frequency of phone calls from this client. Two, we could have realized we were at or nearly past the breaking point when calls dramatically went down two weeks before they cancelled. And three, we are spending 5.6 times as much money on new product development compared to current product maintenance, and only 32.5% of older clients are switching over to newer products. I track this stuff, but no one wants to look at it. It is time for you all to pay attention."

I'm now staring at blank looks from the rest of the leadership. Do they not understand what I am saying? Do I need to make this simpler so they get it? This is so frustrating.…

What contribution is Lisa making, and what unique value does she bring?

What is Lisa overly focused on or attached to that is causing frustration?

THE SCHOLAR'S CONTRIBUTIONS

> I think it's so foolish for people to want to be happy. Happy is so momentary—you're happy for an instant and then you start thinking again. Interest is the most important thing in life; happiness is temporary, but interest is continuous.
>
> *Georgia O'Keeffe*

Scholars are typically all about **knowledge**. They can have an insatiable curiosity that drives them to investigate the how, where and, especially, the why of everything around them. Even if they don't do well academically, Scholars generally process life by gathering information, connecting the dots and synthesizing the data they have collected. They tend to love solving problems and using logic, experimentation and analysis to untangle confusion and find solutions. Scholars can use their large capacity for detail, organization and neutrality to quickly learn and excel in any field, and they often choose, but are not limited to, areas like science, technology, engineering and law. Because Scholars feel compelled to share their knowledge and information, they can also make excellent teachers.

Scholars often love to **gather and organize data** with an emphasis on **accuracy and detail**. During World War II and prior to becoming America's first lady of cooking, Julia Child became the head of the registry of the OSS secretariat in the Far East. Privy to every top-level secret communication, Child was charged with organizing, relaying and tracking sensitive documents and information funneled to and from the OSS. Years later, she carried that drive for accuracy into the creation of her first cookbook, *Mastering the Art of French Cooking*. For ten years, she tested the recipes meticulously and, knowing that ingredients were not the same in the United States as in Europe, she insisted that American cooks of various skill levels test them as well. She approached her television cooking show with a similar organization and precision. Though seemingly casual and informal on camera, Child spent as many as 19 hours preparing for each half-hour segment. She felt strongly that there was a right and wrong way to do things, and, working from detailed notes, she made sure that her instructions and execution were as accurate as possible.

> I'm very much into making lists and breaking things apart into categories.
>
> *David Byrne*

The iconic Scholar, architect Frank Lloyd Wright, was said to have been a driving perfectionist when it came to accuracy and detail. Creating an astounding 1,100 building designs in his lifetime, Wright had an incredible memory for all of the instructions and details he gave to his draftsmen, apprentices and builders on every building design. He had an uncanny ability to catch the slightest mismeasurement or miscalculation. A young apprentice who worked under Wright described him by saying, "Mr. Wright was such a driving perfectionist...with his incessant desire to make everything perfect." The apprentice also said that

Wright had a "remarkable memory" for any instructions he gave. "If we drew a detail that differed the least bit from what he'd asked for, he caught it immediately. He couldn't tolerate the slightest mismeasurement or faulty coordination."

This propensity for accuracy can carry over to a Scholar's strong desire for **precision in communication**. *Precision* here is to be distinguished from *efficient* or *brief*. In general, the Scholar is not necessarily as concerned with communications that pack a lot of punch with few words as they are with making sure that the language is precise. Singer/songwriter Art Garfunkel, of the duo Simon and Garfunkel, is a self-described "thorough, meticulous, disciplined nut." Rather than constantly creating something new, Garfunkel's focus was always on perfecting the execution of the duo's performance and presentation. He was serious about accuracy and repetition, spending hour after hour studying his formations to create a precise sound that expressed the specific meaning of their songs.

Julia Child made sure that her cookbook communicated her intended message by directing the precise way she wanted the book formatted to ensure that no important detail would be overlooked. Her goal was to teach the architecture of her recipes and to make sure that her readers understood each recipe's "alchemical flash points" and potential perils. Therefore, rather than placing all of the ingredients at the beginning of a recipe, she put them within the narrative of the recipe itself, forcing her readers to study each recipe prior to attempting to cook it.

Frank Lloyd Wright's mode of communication was his architectural design. He chose a "grammar" for each building and required that it express a consistent "thought-language" in its design. He insisted that the relationship of all elements be consistent in pattern and flow to the whole. For example, Wright's well-known Martin House used the same brick on the interior as was used on the exterior. Inside the house, Wright added gold leaf in the horizontal joints of the bricks so that they appeared to shimmer like the sun shining. Throughout the house, he used only one type of wood: oak. He used this for everything from the molding and paneling to the doors and furniture in order to communicate a message of precision and unity intended to produce a specific kind of experience for people.

You'll never know everything about anything.

Julia Child

Scholars are often driven to be **thorough** and value **completeness** in their investigations and research. They may continue to dig and ask questions long after others are satisfied. Journalist Diane Sawyer has won several awards for her in-depth journalism, including a report on the crisis in the foster-care system, another on poverty in America and a special that took two years of research in the Appalachian Mountains called "A Hidden America: Children of the Mountains." Her coanchor, Charles Gibson, once remarked, "Diane is much more involved than I am. She'll turn to you when you're about to do an interview and say, 'Are you going to ask about such-and-such?'" Sawyer's producers are reportedly accustomed to getting emails at 2:00 a.m. with her latest findings and areas she wishes to investigate further.

> When I wasn't at school, I was experimenting at home, and became a bit of a Mad Scientist. I did hours of research on mayonnaise, for instance, and though no one else seemed to care about it, I thought it was utterly fascinating...By the end of my research, I believe, I had written more on the subject of mayonnaise than anyone in history.
>
> *Julia Child*

Scholars can be intensely **curious**. They usually love to **investigate, understand how things work** and **solve puzzles**. Jane Goodall, the world's foremost expert on chimpanzees, is best known for her 45-year study of the social and family interactions of wild chimpanzees in Gombe, Tanzania, but her fascination with live animals began at a very young age. "One of my earliest recollections is of the day that I hid in a small stuffy henhouse in order to see how a hen laid an egg. I emerged after about five hours. The whole household had apparently been searching for me for hours, and Mother had even rung the police to report me missing." Later, after Goodall was found and the excitement had passed, she sat down with her mother to explain, in true Scholar fashion, exactly how a hen lays an egg.

> The most fun is getting paid to learn things.
>
> *Diane Sawyer*

When Scholars aren't involved in a subject worthy of their curiosity, they will tend to keep their curiosity alive by **finding other interests**. Before newswoman and anchor Diane Sawyer came into her own, she spent three years as a local "weathergirl" and a part-time reporter. During that time, to satisfy her intellectual curiosity, she attended a semester of law school at night. Of that time, Sawyer said, "It's not gracious to think of law school as an amusement, but it was a perfect antidote to what I was doing during the day. I did find the cases fascinating…like soap opera with a consequence."

> Yeah, I like to keep myself interested—I'll kind of throw myself into some area that I don't completely know or understand, that I'm not adept at, so I'm forced to swim in order to stay afloat. There's a good feeling that comes from that.
>
> *David Byrne*

The curiosity of a Scholar often leads them to ask **constant and insightful questions** of the world around them. Commentator Andy Rooney was known for his odd yet intriguing questions. Touted as the Man of a Thousand Questions, Rooney consistently asked and attempted to answer classics like: "Can you cry under water? How important does a person have to be before they are considered assassinated instead of just murdered? How is it that we put man on the moon before we figured out it would be a good idea to put wheels on luggage? Why is it that people say they 'slept like a baby' when babies wake up like every two hours? In winter why do we try to keep the house as warm as it was in summer when we complained about the heat?"

Well-developed Scholars can also be particularly skilled at **analysis**. They are often able to **discover connections** and **interpret data** then **map** it together and reveal **meaning**. Paul DePodesta, the Harvard economics graduate and inspiration for the analytical genius character in the popular movie *Moneyball*, revolutionized the game of baseball by using statistical analysis versus conventional scouting methods to choose players. DePodesta used the principles of sabermetrics—the empirical analysis of baseball statistics that measure in-game activity—to provide data that was then interpreted and mapped to reveal which players would most likely have their team win. This often led to unconventional choices that drew a lot of questions and criticism. In 1999, he was hired by Billy Beane, the general manager for the ailing Oakland Athletics, as his assistant. DePodesta was described by the *Washington Post* as "a numbers-crunching whiz kid who provided the blueprint for Beane's then revolutionary approach. Utilizing sabermetrics, he helped Beane acquire players who helped Oakland reach the playoffs five times in an eight-year span that ended in 2006."

DePodesta saw his gift for statistical analysis and his ability to glean meaning from data as a way to bring a level of certainty to what is, by nature, unpredictable. DePodesta stated that baseball executives are "constantly trying to predict the future performance of human beings. We're trying to get our arms around that uncertainty. Scouts really help you deal with that uncertainty. On the other hand, we looked at it and said, 'How can we further decrease that uncertainty?' And being able to use data was one of the ways we could do that." With his analytical prowess, DePodesta was able to put sabermetrics into the spotlight of national baseball, produce outstanding results in the process and become a literal game changer on how scouting (and the money spent on players) is viewed.

> I love the early process of asking questions about a story and deciding which questions matter most.
>
> *Diane Sawyer*

Using their **fine-tuned logic**, Scholars can usually **spot what is missing** and get right to the bottom line. In 2008, Senator Elizabeth Warren served as chair of the Congressional Oversight Panel created to oversee the Troubled Asset Relief Program (TARP). Though few people outside Wall Street understood the complexities of various financial instruments such as CDOs and credit-default swaps, Warren had analyzed those vehicles and understood them as well as any of the top players. As a result of her depth of knowledge, Warren was able to grill government officials and demand more accountability from banks and financial institutions. She could pinpoint what was missing in their statements that might normally escape others amid jargon and could see clearly the holes in the logic of their responses. *Vanity Fair* characterized her work by stating, "She held public hearings that were televised, asking the questions that many taxpayers wanted asked—and questions that bankers and Treasury officials did not want to answer."

> Get [in] the habit of analysis—analysis will in time enable synthesis to become your habit of mind.
>
> *Frank Lloyd Wright*

In their analysis of data and quest for information, Scholars can maintain a **neutral objectivity**. As an expert in bankruptcy, Elizabeth Warren conducted a study of personal bankruptcies in the United States and published a book on her findings in 2005. In a 2007 interview, Warren said, "I set out to prove they were all a bunch of cheaters. I was going to expose these people who were taking advantage of the rest of us." But after conducting one of the most rigorous bankruptcy studies ever conducted with two of her colleagues, Warren admitted that she was wrong. The study showed that the vast majority of people who ended up in bankruptcy court were from hardworking, middle-class families who had lost their jobs or had experienced devastating medical setbacks and expenses. Without Warren's natural gift of neutrality in this situation, she could not have opened our eyes the way she did, especially when dealing with an emotionally charged and controversial subject like personal bankruptcy.

THE SCHOLAR UNDERBELLY

Scholars can get **lost within their own heads** and become **enamored with their own theories** to the point that their **internal map becomes more important** than the reality of the situation. They may forget to look outside themselves to what is really happening. Frank Lloyd Wright preferred and repeatedly used a particular aesthetic form for his roofs; yet, he refused to recognize that it did not function. The problem was that even though the design looked stunning and was aesthetically flawless, the roof kept leaking!

> I decided to accept as true my own thinking.
> *Georgia O'Keeffe*

Beyond maintaining their neutrality, Scholars can become stuck in **observing life** while **avoiding participating** in it. They keep their distance and **don't express** or even have **opinions** about what they observe. Many Scholars grew up like famed artist Georgia O'Keeffe, who, even as a child, preferred to be quiet and introspective. She was said to be much more attentive to studying her material surroundings, especially colors and objects, as opposed to engaging in personal relationships. O'Keeffe remained reclusive throughout her life, once admitting, "I find people very difficult."

Scholars are often accused of being **emotionless, impersonal** and **cold**. Georgia O'Keeffe's marriage to photographer Alfred Stieglitz was described by her biographer as "a collusion…a system of deals and trade-offs, tacitly agreed to and carried out, for the most part, without the exchange of a word." When O'Keeffe saw nude photographs that her husband had taken of her, she said, "I felt somehow that the photographs had nothing to do with me personally."

In a similar way, Scholars prefer ordinary reality to drama and make-believe. In an interview, Andy Rooney talked about preferring his own world: "I don't go to many movies. I don't read many novels. I—it's strange, and I have tried to analyze it. But I am so—I enjoy my own life. I am so interested in the realness in my own life that I am not interested in being carried away into somebody else's world in a novel or in a movie."

Less-developed Scholars tend to **lack awareness of social politics**, and they often **do not understand or are oblivious to others' feelings**. In 1994, commentator Andy Rooney made several insensitive remarks about Kurt Cobain's suicide, such as, "What's all this nonsense about how terrible life is?" and "If [Cobain] applied the same brain to his music that he applied to his drug-infested life, it's reasonable to think that his music may not have made much sense either." Two years earlier, Rooney wrote that it was "silly" for Native Americans to complain about team names like the Redskins. "The real problem is, we took the country away from the Indians, they want it back and we're not going to give it to them. We feel guilty and we'll do what we can for them within reason, but they can't have their country back." Even in his public apologies after these incidents, Rooney never seemed to grasp why his words had been so hurtful.

....

> I don't very much enjoy looking at
> paintings in general. I know too much
> about them. I take them apart.
> *Georgia O'Keeffe*

....

Scholars have a tendency to feel **superior** and think they are
smarter than everyone around them. They can unintentionally be
arrogant and **harshly critical**. Critics of Elizabeth Warren, likely
non-Scholars, accused her of such arrogance, saying, "How dare
this woman criticize the free-enterprise system?" They perceived
it as unimaginable that someone new to an area could so quickly
and so thoroughly understand something so complex.

In an interview, Frank Lloyd Wright stated, "I've been accused of
saying I was the greatest architect in the world and if I had said
so, I don't think it would be very arrogant, because I don't believe
there are many [great architects]—if any. For 500 years what we
call architecture has been phony."

Scholars can be intellectual snobs, and they often know it. Scholars may also be the ones who are sticklers for credentials, and
not just any credentials, but the right ones. It is not so much that
people have been to the best schools, but they ought to have been
somewhere that required them to think. Scholar executives may
refuse to hire anyone who can't demonstrate what is to them a
minimum level of intellectual achievement. To non-Scholars, this
typically seems like holding the academic bar too high, especially

for positions that don't require this amount of formal education.

> Early in my career...I had to choose between
> an honest arrogance and a hypercritical
> humility...I deliberately choose an honest
> arrogance, and I've never been sorry.
> *Frank Lloyd Wright*

OTHER SCHOLAR CHARACTERISTICS

Less-developed Scholars can get caught up in an **excessive need for data**. They may freeze, **unable to decide** or act without mountains of data, which blocks or slows momentum for the projects they are working on. They might continue to ask questions long after a conclusion has been reached and can be slow to release their original theories unless undeniably proven wrong. They can **lose themselves in detail, unable to discern what is important** and what is irrelevant. They are often pedantic in presenting their findings and **overly serious** in their approach to life.

Scholars can also have a strange, **quirky sense of humor** that only other Scholars understand. Being more **literal** than symbolic in their communication, they tend to miss or misunderstand sarcasm and other subtle forms of humor. They are typically less aware of their bodies and tend to be **physically awkward**.

SCHOLAR STAGES OF DEVELOPMENT

STAGE 1: Scholars in Stage 1 tend to be enthralled with information for information's sake. Though inordinately determined in their quest for increasing amounts of data, their understanding of the data they gather is superficial. These Scholars don't yet appreciate the difference between facts and meaning or even the relative importance of the data they jealously hoard (competing for the most and best information). Their approach to problem solving is to overwhelm with facts and figures, augmenting the difficulty of the problem. They tend to hoard and then dump their vast quantities of detail and even trivia on those around them. In research, Stage 1 Scholars tend to stick to a tried and true, systematic approach. They are suspicious of approaches that appear messy, unstructured or consist of outside-the-box thinking and tend to emphasize theory while ignoring or avoiding reality.

Scholars in this stage tend to become paralyzed and unable to act. They get lost in their heads, and, overwhelmed by massive quantities of details, they easily lose sight of the ultimate destination or goal. Thinking that more data will reveal solutions, they seek more and more information before they believe they can make a decision. Stage 1 Scholars are often harsh in their criticism of others when they feel the data is incomplete. Lacking the ability to connect the dots of the information they have gathered, these Scholars focus on increasing their memory capacity and enhancing intellectual structures to organize their data.

To move forward, Scholars in Stage 1 need to distinguish between data that is relevant and data that is not. They need to be encouraged to understand the importance of the information they possess and to help others understand it as well. Beyond memorizing facts and figures, these Scholars can be coached to think about the data and analyze its meaning with regard to the issues or problems involved. To open them to doing this, coach them to see that they contribute even when they don't know everything.

STAGE 2: Scholars at this stage have a better understanding of the relative importance of the data they collect. But while they understand this data on a micro level, they still are unable to connect this information effectively on a macro level. They are still attached to finding flaws in others' arguments and positions, and they can be very assertive in foisting their findings on those around them. Because they can now map information, albeit on the micro level, they are acutely aware of what data is wrong or missing, and they are driven to point this out. Stage 2 Scholars love logic, precision and clarity and feel superior to others because of their pure intellectual perspective.

Stage 2 Scholars emphasize the supreme value of neutral observation and can be overly serious. They believe that participation, especially participation that includes emotions, will contaminate their perception and pollute the scientific methodology they prefer to use in testing their theories. This attitude leads Scholars to ignore people's feelings and motivations. They still prefer theory over reality and live life through what they understand in their minds rather than through direct experience.

Stage 2 Scholars can benefit by loosening up and learning to take themselves and their data less seriously. To expand their capacity, they must begin to see the value of participating and making emotional connections rather than staying completely on the sidelines and in their heads. When they don't participate, prompt them by asking them to consider what they don't know. They also can be coached to appreciate what others have to offer that they may be missing, rather than focusing on how their current understanding and awareness is better than what others know. Even if they don't have all the data or intellectual clarity they would prefer, Stage 2 Scholars can be encouraged to be more effective by making decisions and moving forward in what are best called "experiments."

STAGE 3: Scholars in this stage are much more accepting of people and have developed a healthy neutrality with and detachment from the information they collect. They are much more able to see subtleties and the truth behind information; they question the validity of new data and also revise their own theories based on what they experience. These Scholars can now also analyze their findings and connect the dots within the framework of a bigger picture perspective. They quickly make extensive intellectual maps that deliver meaning. Rather than information for its own sake, Stage 3 Scholars have fine-tuned their sense of what data is relevant and how much is needed for decision-making and taking action.

Scholars in this stage are also becoming more attuned to and appreciative of the "soft elements" of human experience, and they are more willing to participate in the "messiness" of human interaction. They are becoming holistic thinkers, more comfortable and confident with their own knowing. Rather than dumping what they know on others, these Scholars now encourage others' curiosity and exploration. They have become skilled traditional problem solvers via their expansive knowledge, their skills at discovering information and their heightened ability to analyze information to connect the dots in figurative maps and unearth meaning.

Stage 3 Scholars are ready to turn their knowledge into a broader wisdom. They can be encouraged to alternate their focus on detail to the broader picture, to emphasize the macro rather than the micro. By doing so, they will be able to reach deeper understandings and increase their influence to a wider audience. These Scholars are also ready to trust their immediate knowing and to explore their intuition. To do this, they need to process not only with their intellects, but also with emphasis on their hearts and bodies. Ask these Scholars how they'd know more if they used all their knowing. Challenge them to explain things such as intuition that they have likely seen others use successfully. Help them see how the deepest and best learning can be messy.

STAGE 4: Scholars in Stage 4 have come fully into their power. They have incorporated mind, body and heart, and are willing to fully participate in the "messy experiment" that is life. Because they are fully engaged in each moment, they have a deep clarity and awareness, a type of interactive knowing that is immediate and naturally flows with the situation. These Scholars have the ability to synthesize and integrate multiple perspectives with ease. People are drawn to Stage 4 Scholars because of their accepting neutrality and their ability to simultaneously broaden and refine ideas and theories. Scholars in this stage are ready to move beyond knowledge from others and grow their own body of knowledge.

Rather than mere intellectual knowing, these Scholars are drawn to wisdom and truth, and they understand that truth is not absolute but fluid in each moment. They have learned to trust their intuition and understand their unique gift is in spontaneous discovery and that mastery is in giving up mastering. Stage 4 Scholars also understand that the importance of wisdom is not in having it but in what they are able to do with it. They focus now on helping others to recognize and trust their own knowing and discovery process.

SCHOLAR SWEET SPOT—KEY POINTS

CORE VALUES & BEHAVIORS
- accuracy, details, knowledge, completeness
- research, investigation, experimentation, curiosity, asking questions
- neutrality, objectivity
- solving puzzles
- analysis, logic, meaning, interpretation, mapping information

TRIGGERS

- wrong or missing information
- poor or absent logic
- ignoring lessons of the past

CHALLENGES

- too much detail, caught in the micro
- lost in their own heads/theories, excessive need for data, inability to decide
- lack of social and political awareness, oblivious to others' feelings
- overly geeky or nerdy
- hard to read—low feeling/emotional presence, cold, impersonal
- observe and don't participate or offer opinions
- arrogant, intellectually superior, harshly critical

GREAT ORGANIZATIONAL ROLES

- accounting, finance
- research and development, market research, documentation
- problem solving, engineering, science, IT
- institutional memory
- management, training, law, mediation, psychotherapy

THE SCHOLAR LEADER

- explains their reasoning/rationale backed up by information
- clarifies with step-by-step instructions
- wants to know details or know they're handled by direct reports
- creates a learning culture

TIPS & COACHING:
LEVERAGING YOUR SCHOLAR TALENT

If you discover you've got the Scholar Sweet Spot while reading this chapter, these are ways you can experience the most joy, ease and collaboration and create the best results:

> **Answer complex questions** whenever you can—Scholars love bringing their knowledge together to solve problems and are great at it

- You likely provide the greatest value by sharing the knowledge you've assimilated and integrated—use it and share it generously
- Put yourself in situations in which you can spontaneously answer questions from your holistic, more intuitive knowing, even when you can't explain why you have these answers
- Scholars are particularly great at translating knowledge from one area into the different language and context from which a question might come

> Learn and share **information in balance**—Scholars try to learn more than they need and overshare information when they are nervous

- When exploring a new area, notice if you believe you need to figure it all out before taking action; see how you already know so much more than others in this area and can be of service by taking action much sooner
- Beware of a desire for perfection and absolute accuracy; this

can unnecessarily delay progress

- Tune in to your audience before and during the sharing of information, such as in a meeting or presentation, to see what is really wanted and helpful
- Explore getting more comfortable with the **unknown**, trying things out without instructions or formal training and learning in the moment

> Focus on **the forest, not only the trees**—Scholars can get lost down in the details and need to keep coming back up to the big picture

- Regularly look from a broad view; keep in mind the "why"—ensure the things you are doing and building *now* are growing what you really want *later*
- As you mature in your Scholar Talent and more easily see the bigger picture, hand off details to others
- When accurate details really are important, hire and delegate them to other people with these skills so that you feel comfortable handing this work off

> **Don't rely solely on your "map" and forget about reality**—Scholars can get lost in the theory they know and inadvertently ignore reality

- Look around, literally, to see what is real—one of your gifts is working with maps in your mind in addition to print and virtual maps that model what exists, but don't rely *only* on them (e.g., be sure to also look at the physical world)
- Even though something ought to exist based on a plan (e.g., products in a warehouse, an employee working on a project,

a street on a roadmap), check to see if it really does

> Jump in to **participate**—Scholars learn more and things that are of greater relevance when they are taking action rather than just observing

- Shake up your fear of "contaminating" the data; get in there and experiment
- Share your opinions, not just facts, even when you can't fully explain why you see something a particular way—your view is valuable because you naturally integrate many perspectives together

> Explore the realm of **feelings**—this allows a Scholar to access more of their wisdom and put it in action

- Learn about basic feelings (e.g., mad, sad, glad, scared, sexual), both in theory and how they show up in your own body
- Get in touch with what you want, simply because you want it and are curious about it, not because it is logical; your Scholar will be more powerful when you follow your own interests
- Connecting with your feelings will allow you to use your entire self as a learning and sleuthing antenna (this is one way you access your intellectual intuition)
- Being able to navigate in the realm of feelings will also allow you to be so much more understandable to other people; they'll be more able to trust you and accept your knowledge

TIPS & COACHING: WORKING WITH A SCHOLAR

If you discover you are managing or working with someone who has the Scholar Sweet Spot:

> **Ask them questions**—answering them is one of their favorite things
  - They love being valued for their knowledge and ability to solve problems; they'll feel seen and appreciated
  - Give them complex, information-rich situations to map and translate for others—it will increase their motivation for all their work
  - Give them productive puzzles to investigate and solve (e.g., "I want to know how to do…Please find out how others do this")
  - Scholars are great at proofreading to find what is missing and wrong, such as what is inconsistent between two related things when computers can't easily compare them (e.g., financial data, copy, and related procedures)

> Encourage them to **share opinions and participate**—not just objectively share facts
  - Scholars start out completely neutral and objective, hence they may not be able to recognize their opinions and realize their value
  - They can learn to open to their opinions by getting in better touch with their feelings and desires, for as they explore this, their opinions will spring to life; suggest they read, take classes, etc.

- Similarly, Scholars often start out observing so as to not contaminate the data they are gathering; encourage them to experiment with participating as a way of learning more and richer information
- Reinforce how valuable their input has been after they've taken risks to participate and share their opinion

> Encourage them to pull back and up to **take a look from a high level**—Scholars can have a tendency to get caught in the weeds

- You may need to be responsible for bringing in a broad perspective at the beginning of each meeting with them, as they may still be excited about details they've been focusing on
- As they learn more about and gain mastery in a subject area, they often naturally broaden their view, so it may be helpful to be a bit patient in the beginning (but do nudge them forward if they get stuck in analysis paralysis)

> Include them in as many **information-sharing experiences** (e.g., meetings, emails) as possible—Scholars feel calmer when "in the know"

- Scholars feel uncomfortable when they don't know enough about what is going on, and they'll feel honored and respected when you take the time to share
- Listen to and use their relevant knowledge from the past—Scholars house institutional knowledge that is valuable
- Scholars automatically absorb data and compare it to what they already know, so when receiving new information, they

always scan it for inaccuracies and gaps that can be very useful to know about

> Encourage them to stretch their edges in being **comfortable with the unknown and taking risks**
  - Calculated (and gut-instinct) risks are essential in business, and Scholars often don't like them
  - A Scholar's inability to work with risk will block their growth in the business if they're not able to move forward with the risk of missing information (e.g., taking steps forward on a project when the details aren't all known)
  - As with all the other Talents, Scholars need to learn to move through fear; particularly, they need to understand that the risk of waiting to get absolute accuracy can be great, causing valuable time to be wasted and a window of opportunity to be missed
  - Encourage them to trust their innate knowing and explore that they don't need formal training when learning to do something new (e.g., they don't need a certification or another academic degree)

> Scholars sometimes **don't fit in as well socially**—they literally need education and training in this area
  - Teach them what behaviors will support others to more easily connect with them and give them opportunities to practice
  - Mentor them (or suggest they take training) on navigating politics, the art of communication, giving presentations, etc.
  - Honor their unusual sense of humor, even if you don't get

it—laugh and ask them what it means, and even then you still may not grok what's funny; encourage them to connect with others who do (Note: if you don't know what *grok* means, ask your local Scholar)

FAMOUS SCHOLARS

Alex Haley	Indira Gandhi	Paul Simon
Andy Rooney	James Cronin	Raymond Davis
Art Garfunkel	Jane Goodall	Rebecca Armstrong
Christine Lagarde	John Malkovich	Ruth Ann Marshall
Dan Rather	Julia Child	Stanley Kramer
David Byrne	Lauren Bacall	Susan Arnold
Diane Sawyer	Leonard Nimoy	Ted Koppel
Elizabeth Warren	Leonardo da Vinci	Tip O'Neil
Ennio Morricone	Margaret Mead	Tom Brokaw
Georgia O'Keeffe	Mark Zuckerberg	Tom Landry
Gertrude Anscombe	Marshall McLuhan	Tom Peters
Glen Seaborg	M. C. Escher	Warren Burger
Harry Reasoner	Mike Wallace	William Petersen
Harry Reid	Newt Gingrich	

CHAPTER 7

THE KING

KEVIN, VICE PRESIDENT OF MARKETING

Day of GlobalApp's corporate retreat:

Of course I missed breakfast—there really was nothing to be gained from chatting with people over muffins. This meeting, though, could prove very useful. I'm not interested in hashing out why we lost a "key" client. I say move on. We don't need them. Let's find bigger, better clients. What I am interested in, however, is the opportunity to figure out how these people operate—what I can learn about them that will ultimately help me build GlobalApp's empire and my own empire as well.

Dave just revealed that he has a really tight relationship with the client we just lost. I wonder if that bridge is now burned or if I can persuade him to salvage any other good connections from them, especially if it is one of our untapped markets.

I've positioned myself to be the last one to speak—this way I know what I'm dealing with and can change my approach as needed. There's so much going on here—both said and unsaid—that I can use to strategize. "Kevin," says Brian, "what are your thoughts?

What is the biggest problem GlobalApp has to solve?" I pause and give it a few moments before speaking. "We are not taking advantage of the opportunities that we could be," I say. "We still aren't poised to crush the competition the way we have the power to. Losing a client here and there will be par for the course when we dominate the market. We can't afford to get too concerned about individual clients even now—we have to maintain an attitude of being a large-scale player, not a mom-and-pop shop that frets over every lost customer."

I can sense some of the other leaders bristling at this remark. I don't mind this. Many of these leaders, as talented as they are, just can't see the bigger strategy here. They focus on building a boat when I'm out to have my team build a fleet of several thousand ships. But it's definitely beneficial to see their reactions. I'll use this to strategize down the road....

What contribution is Kevin making, and what unique value does he bring?

What is Kevin overly focused on or attached to that is causing frustration?

THE KING'S CONTRIBUTIONS

Though less than 3% of the population has any natural King Talent, Kings can make a **powerful impact** on the world, an impact that far outweighs their numbers. (Because King Talent is so rare, we have included some famous examples who have King as their 2nd or 3rd Talent, and a few of them appear in other chapters as well.) Whether as CEO, prime minister or head of the marketing department, well-developed Kings can be courageous and resourceful with a solid, charismatic presence. They have a tendency to willingly take responsibility for producing results and naturally seek the most effective means to outcomes that will have the biggest impact and build their power. A King who has come fully into their own will radiate a calmness, clarity, commitment and certainty that inspires others to follow them, whether it be to wage war, launch new technologies or land on the moon.

Kings tend to be **powerful leaders** because they can be no other way. Kings like Pablo Picasso clearly recognized this innate quality in themselves: "My mother said to me, 'If you are a soldier, you will become a general. If you are a priest, you will become Pope.' Instead, I was a painter, and I became Picasso." They are likely to carry themselves with the natural and unmistakable air of **authority**, even **majesty**. Kings can bring a **decisive, totally confident** form of leadership that is driven by their **single focus**. Although at times people might prefer a more democratic or collaborative type of leadership, Kings typically **follow their own internal compass** and can be invaluable leaders in crisis. People tend to gain strength from a King's unwavering certainty and often feel relieved, reassured and grateful when a King steps in to take charge and tell them what to do, where to go and how to get there.

The Iron Lady of Israel, Golda Meir, who served as Israeli prime minister from 1969 to 1974, exhibited that certainty throughout her career, but particularly when catastrophe seemed imminent. Historians claim that, unlike other Israeli leaders, Meir had no trouble making decisions during times of crisis. Chaim Herzog (who became Israel's sixth president in 1983) was critical of her leadership at the start of the Yom Kippur War. However, he said, "Once the war began, she showed great strength of character and enormous composure…her inflexibility proved to be an enormous asset in the war. She used common sense to make military decisions, often opposing the choices made by lifelong military men—and her choices were usually correct."

> Singleness of purpose is one of the chief essentials for success in life, no matter what may be one's aim.
>
> *J. D. Rockefeller*

Winston Churchill (King is his 2nd Talent) exemplified this decisive quality during the difficult early days of World War II. While other British leaders waffled and worried, Churchill refused to consider defeat or any action that would compromise his nation's sovereignty. His confidence and staunch determination helped inspire the British population to actively oppose Nazi Germany, despite the fact that this tiny nation stood alone while other countries gave in to Hitler's demands and followed courses of appeasement.

Kings do not usually struggle or strain to accomplish their great achievements. Instead, it is their **strong will** that can impel their projects and plans forward. In general, a King's grand plan isn't meant to stay on the drawing board. When they focus their tremendous will toward a particular outcome, no matter how large or expansive, they are likely to be fully confident that it will **take form in reality**. With a **fearlessness** that is both inspiring and intimidating, they may announce, "It shall be so," with the implicit message of "No matter what!"

> One reason so few of us achieve what we truly want is that we never direct our focus; we never concentrate our power. Most people dabble their way through life, never deciding to master anything in particular.
>
> *Tony Robbins*

As a child in Milwaukee, Golda Meir was a bright student. But her parents were determined that her education would end after eighth grade so that she could be married. Meir rebelled and enrolled in a public high school in 1912, paying for her supplies by working various jobs. Her parents tried to force her to quit school and began to search for her future husband. At 14, Meir contacted her sister, who lived in Denver with her new husband, and convinced her to send train fare. One morning, Meir pretended to head for school but instead boarded a train. She returned a few years later when her parents agreed she could complete high school. When she finally decided she was ready to marry, Meir insisted on a precondition to her engagement—that her future husband agree to settle in Palestine and live in a kibbutz. Through her fierce will and fearlessness, Meir propelled her life forward in the direction she was certain she wanted to go.

Speaker and life coach Tony Robbins had a difficult and violent childhood. Surrounded by uncertainty, he says, "I pounded certainty into myself. I literally conditioned myself to be certain, to have that confidence, that strength, and it was something I did by controlling my mind." He basically "willed" himself into certainty. By high school, classmates described him as "Mr. Solution," and his goal was to be president. As a young teenager, he bristled against his mother's rules and stormed out of the house, saying that he was "too powerful" to live with his mother any longer. He worked as a janitor while living with a friend, and when his mother tried to cut off all sources of assistance to him, he quit school and found a sales position. At 17, after being introduced to entrepreneur and motivational speaker, Jim Rohn, Robbins asked Rohn for a job. Fearless in his desire to guide the direction of his own life and having an unyielding will to succeed, Robbins quickly mastered Rohn's program, and, by age 19, he was making $10,000 per month and would go on to dominate the world of personal growth.

> Strength does not come from physical capacity.
> It comes from an indomitable will.
> *Mahatma Gandhi*

Kings can speak with such an assuredness and confidence that **others tend to follow**. When they propose an idea, people rarely question it; they simply line up and get started. People typically get on board quickly, and the King usually makes it clear in some way that if you are not on board, they have little use for you. Beginning in the 1980s, pop icon Madonna presented herself with such brash boldness and confidence that much of the American public came to believe she was an authority on cutting-edge trends, and she compelled the culture to follow her. In an interview on American Bandstand in 1984, Madonna was asked by Dick Clark about her main ambition. "I have the same goal I've had ever since I was a girl: **I want to rule the world**." Madonna saw herself as having similar power and ambition to Argentina's Evita. She is said to have been so confident she was a fit for the upcoming film role of Evita that she sent a handwritten letter to the director explaining why she was perfect for the part. As is typical of people dealing with Kings, the director followed her lead and gave her the part, despite the outrage voiced by many Argentinian citizens.

As Madonna stated so clearly, **Kings want to rule**. This does not always show up in a tyrannical manner (of which we have countless examples in history—think Mao Tse-tung), but they often have a gift for getting people on board with their ideas. And not with just any ideas, but with **seemingly outrageous ideas** that might normally seem far too big or too impossible in scope to actually achieve. People often think they are "crazy" for thinking they could make something that enormous happen, but coming from the King, they somehow respect the idea, are willing to follow and want to be on board in case it does really work. People seem to be compelled to be a part of their plan. In 1962, John F. Kennedy (King is his 2nd Talent) compelled the nation to get behind the idea of putting a man on the moon. He proclaimed, "No nation which expects to be the leader of other nations can expect to stay behind in this race for space. We choose to go to the Moon in this decade and do the other things, not because they are easy, but because they are hard; because that goal will serve to organize and measure the best of our energies and skills; because that challenge is one that we are willing to accept, one we are unwilling to postpone, and one which we intend to win." Even though there were plenty of people who had their doubts about something that, at the time, seemed beyond impossible, Kennedy was able to get the nation as a whole on board.

> There is no such thing as failure.
> There are only results.
> *Tony Robbins*

Kings can be **master strategists** with an **extraordinary sense of timing,** knowing exactly when to direct actions for maximum benefit and impact. Mahatma Gandhi was such a King. Several times during the decades when he led the effort to free India from British rule, he called off major campaigns of civil disobedience that were threatening to turn violent. He knew that violence would undermine the entire process, damage international support and ignite retaliation from the British. He planned campaigns carefully for times when nonviolent noncooperation could be maintained.

I must govern the clock, not be governed by it.
Golda Meir

Kings are typically able to see **big opportunities** that others miss, often using existing knowledge, inventions or technologies, but bringing them together in a unique and powerful way that often creates a totally **new paradigm**. Henry Ford developed the assembly-line technique of mass production that produced affordable automobiles and caused a paradigm shift that revolutionized American travel and culture. Ford also instituted the unheard of practice of paying his workers high wages—which not only eliminated turnover and absenteeism, but also created a new class of consumers who could afford his cars. He saw paying higher wages as an enormous opportunity in an era when most would have seen this as financial waste.

If you want to succeed, you should strike out on new paths, rather than travel the worn paths of accepted success.
John D. Rockefeller

Madonna also exemplified someone who saw big opportunities and shifted paradigms. She is well known in the industry for being a marketing genius when it comes to recognizing and seizing opportunities—from being one of the first pop stars to take advantage of the game-changing power of the music video to turning the public scrutiny of her sexuality into an overt power play with her book, *Sex*. In addition to creating a paradigm shift in fashion that girls all over the country imitated (fishnet stockings, lace lingerie, fingerless gloves and large crucifix necklaces), she has managed to consistently take advantage of controversy as an opportunity to expand her power in the media, increase her empire and, more recently, bring causes she wants to champion to light.

> To succeed in business it is necessary to make others see things as you see them.
> *Aristotle Onassis*

A King can have the power and **charismatic presence** to **lead and orchestrate very large groups** of people, exhorting them to go above and beyond their own expectations and fears. Mahatma Gandhi is a prime example. Before the days of Twitter and with little in the way of reliable communication technology, Gandhi was able to organize millions of followers, literate and illiterate, from diverse religions and all class structures, convincing even the most radical factions to support "peaceful noncooperation" as the means to secure an independent India. John F. Kennedy inspired a whole generation to action when he said, "My fellow

Americans, ask not what your country can do for you, ask what you can do for your country." With those words in 1961, he launched the Peace Corps. Within five years, over 15,000 young Americans were volunteering in developing countries throughout the world, countering the growing stereotype of Yankee Imperialism and the "Ugly American." Both Gandhi and JFK were able to mobilize large groups to do things that were outside the norm for people, beyond what was predictable in their day-to-day lives, believing that they could make a difference. These Kings were not intimidated by the big machines they were facing—British rule, the American system of complacency—thereby having those who followed them believe these systems were not impenetrable and not impossible to change as well.

Kings also tend to be keenly attuned to the need for **"clearing the playing field"—demolishing prior solutions, approaches or structures** to wipe the slate clean and make way for superior methods. To bring their larger plan into being, they are willing to completely dismantle organizations, reject old rules of engagement and ignore conventional wisdom.

> Failure is simply the opportunity to begin again, this time more intelligently.
> *Henry Ford*

Margaret Thatcher became notorious for her willingness to clear the playing field. According to *The Economist*, once she was in power, "government spending was curbed to control the money supply, while currency was allowed to float [rather than joining the new European Monetary System], both decisive breaks with postwar orthodoxies. Industrial subsidies were cut, sending many firms to the wall." At one point, Thatcher became the most unpopular prime minister on record, and, while her own colleagues tried to persuade her that her choices were unwise, she was unmoved. Ministers who wanted her to do a U-turn and reverse her policy changes were cleared out. *The Economist* went on to say that Thatcher "sacked all those ministers, the 'wets,' who wanted to change course, and stocked her cabinet with ideological fellow-travellers." To make way for privatization, she proceeded to demolish the accepted structure of huge companies such as British Telecom, British Gas, and British Airways being government owned. In perhaps her most well-known act of tearing down prior structures, she abolished the powerful grip of the National Union of Mineworkers. After a tumultuous showdown, her victory "broke the unions for good," making way for what she felt was a far more effective form of management.

Whereas Thatcher focused on wiping the slate clean externally, Tony Robbins dominated his industry by focusing on wiping the slate clean internally. Robbins asserts that great personal achievement can only happen after one's internal limiting beliefs have been eradicated and new positive beliefs installed. He says, "What we can or cannot do, what we consider possible or impossible, is rarely a function of our true capability. It is more likely a function of our beliefs about who we are." Using tenets of neuro-linguistic programming, he has taught over four million people from around the world the importance of destroying old negative beliefs in order to clear out space to adopt new ones and, in the process, made way for his own successful empire in what was then an emerging market.

Every act of creation is first an act of destruction.

Pablo Picasso

THE KING UNDERBELLY

Though people appreciate their Kings when crisis hits, and we value their powerful, groundbreaking contributions, Kings can also be difficult. They can exude an absolute confidence and will-fulness that can be interpreted as **arrogance**, and they may come across as if they see themselves as superior to those around them. As Katharine Hepburn described her sense of self, "Most people are brought up to believe they are as good as the person next to them. I was told I was better."

Do you think I am going to hang around this piddling town? For me, the whole world is small. I don't need any diploma. You will marvel one day at what I shall do.

Aristotle Onassis

"Often wrong, never in doubt" is a phrase that can aptly describe Kings. Their internal compass is typically strong, and they know what they know, so their opinions are often expressed as absolute truths rather than merely personal beliefs. Their tendency toward extreme self-confidence in their ideas can come across as **inflexible** and can be off-putting. Kings like Madonna will simply say, "Everyone is entitled to my opinion." A *Reuters* article after Margaret Thatcher's death acknowledged that she was equally revered and loathed. As one interviewee put it, "I found her to be confrontational, dogmatic, abrasive; she attacked people in her own country and didn't listen to people in her own party. She was destructive, nihilistic."

A King's majestic vision can seem **grandiose and self-serving**. Even Kings whose goals focus on service to mankind can appear to be **narcissistic**, especially to those who don't agree with those goals. Contemporaries of Mahatma Gandhi described him as an "opportunist" who used theatrics that played to short-lived outcomes and crowd-pleasing themes. Historians critical of John F. Kennedy accused him of overreacting during the Cuban Missile Crisis and bringing the world to the brink of nuclear war merely to prove himself to be a strong leader before midterm elections in November. Field Marshall Alan Brooke, who was on Winston Churchill's General Staff, wrote about the prime minister in his diary in 1944: "And the wonderful thing is that 3/4 of the population of the world imagine that Churchill is one of the Strategists of History, a second Marlborough, and the other 1/4 have no idea what a public menace he is and has been throughout this war! It is far better that the world should never know, and never suspect the feet of clay of this otherwise superhuman being. Without him England was lost for a certainty, with him England has been on the verge of disaster time and again…Never have I admired and despised a man simultaneously to the same extent. Never have such opposite extremes been combined in the same human being."

Kings are usually certain of their own ideas and plans and are typically **not collaborative** in their approach. People around a King can rarely influence their singleness of purpose or direction because the King's internal compass trumps all outside influence. At best, Kings may invite others to provide expertise and honest opinions on how a project could be accomplished but rarely on the likely success of the project itself. At their worst, Kings may leave no space for others to express their ideas or opinions at any level. As Prime Minister Thatcher described it, "I don't mind how much my Ministers talk, so long as they do what I say." In addition to rarely being collaborative, Kings can sometimes see people simply as pawns in their grand schemes, and this can be exactly how people feel around them. As long as their followers are competent enough to make things happen, Kings are usually happy enough to have them participate; if not competent, those people often become irrelevant. Alfred Hitchcock was infamous for his treatment of actors, describing them as "cattle" and "animated props."

Well, I don't know [that] I want a lawyer to tell me what I cannot do. I hire him to tell me how I can do what I want to do.

J.P. Morgan

Should a person be deemed incompetent in the King's eyes, not only are they likely to occur as irrelevant, but Kings become intolerant. Rarely providing second chances to people who are untruthful or who don't keep their commitments, Kings generally have no patience for people who can't get tasks or projects accomplished—and they are not usually interested in hearing excuses. Many Kings subscribe to the "off with their heads" form of management.

A King often has a naturally assertive (even aggressive) physical presence, emanating a powerful energy that can feel intimidating, and they can be ruthless in pursuit of their goals. Many Kings would agree with Katharine Hepburn: "Why slap them on the wrist with a feather when you can belt them over the head with a sledgehammer?" In his book *Guts*, auto executive Bob Lutz said in reference to his eighth immutable law of business, "When you inherit a really big rat's nest, don't try to lure them out with food. Use a flamethrower!" In addition to treating his actors like "props," Alfred Hitchcock was said to have ruthlessly manipulated their contracts to get the results he desired.

Kings tend to be turf builders. As such, they typically avoid other Kings and the turf of other Kings. Instead, they often determine where their own turf lies (talent, industry, expertise or mission) and set out to own that turf by being the best and most prominent within it. At an early age, John D. Rockefeller determined that his turf was oil. By the time he was 33, he controlled 90% of the North American oil supply by first intimidating then buying out his competitors and creating the first monopoly. Rockefeller then built a 4,000-mile pipeline to deliver his oil to break his company's dependence on the railroads, which were controlled by two others attempting to build turf, Cornelius Vanderbilt and Tom Scott.

Though extroverted when gathering and directing followers, on a personal level, Kings are often accused of being **aloof**. They typically don't engage with the smaller, day-to-day problems that most people focus on and can't relate to others' worries about mundane concerns. Kings often feel **isolated**, which they accept as a natural consequence of living in the lofty place from which they perceive and operate. As Margaret Thatcher expressed it, "Being prime minister is a lonely job…you cannot lead from the crowd."

OTHER KING CHARACTERISTICS

Kings tend to be extremely **ambitious**, but, in general, their motivation is not just to gain celebrity. They typically don't quest for power for its own sake but yearn to express the power they feel they already have. In accomplishing goals and grand projects that they deem worthy, Kings can be **intensely directed** and **doggedly persistent**. Winston Churchill asserted, "One ought never to turn one's back on a threatened danger and try to run away from it. If you do that, you will double the danger. But if you meet it promptly and without flinching, you will reduce the danger by half. Never run away from anything. Never!" With an eye on the goal, they tend to meet obstacles on their path with their sheer will and confidence and often ignore the rules if those rules impede progress. For the most part, their internal compass is the only law they insist on honoring.

> Being powerful is like being a lady.
> If you have to tell people you are, you aren't.
> *Margaret Thatcher*

On the flip side of despising incompetence, Kings usually place a high value on **mastery**. They can have an exceptional ability to identify the best people and resources to implement their plan, and they surround themselves with people who are masters within their disciplines. Kings tend to hold themselves to a high standard of performance and expect everyone within their circle to hold to that same standard. Kings often insist on **integrity**— that people around them do what they say they will do, when they say they will do it. They are likely to demand that people around them voice their authentic opinions, and only respect those who fully express their **principles in both word and deed**. As Mahatma Gandhi said, "To believe in something, and not to live it, is dishonest."

> I believe in the sacredness of a promise,
> that a man's word should be as good as
> his bond, that character—not wealth or
> power or position—is of supreme worth.
> *John D. Rockefeller*

KING STAGES OF DEVELOPMENT

STAGE 1: Kings in this stage, to put it mildly, are not very likeable. They act like dictators, using the intimidation of a gang leader to coerce their minions into fulfilling their desires. Overbearing and verbally (if not physically) abusive, their attitude toward others is condescending and dismissive. Stage 1 Kings rule by insulting, shaming and terrorizing others. They are intolerant of weakness, and they will destroy simply for destruction's sake, rather than breaking down something as a means to build something better.

Kings at this stage are a handful and difficult to incorporate on any team or within any business unit. To coach them, it's important to remind them that their desire is true power, not temporary or unsustainable power, and that they will be more successful if their followers are strong, not weakened by abuse and intimidation. A King can be coached to choose people worthy of fighting their battles. A King shows that they are moving to the next stage when they have the confidence to choose stronger followers and show respect for their team members as human beings.

STAGE 2: These Kings share many of the characteristics of Kings in Stage 1 but are slightly less brazen and destructive. They are still demanding and controlling of others and establish their power by force, constantly fighting for turf. No matter the outcome of these battles, they present themselves as victorious, appearing vain and self-aggrandizing. In dealing with enemies and followers, these Kings can still be heartless, abrupt and explosive. They fear weakness of any sort, in themselves or their team. Despite this, they are successful at building an empire of resources and having their people accomplish great feats of increasing magnitude.

Kings at this stage are still difficult to have within a business setting. To help them move to the next stage, they should be reminded that they are powerful naturally and that their deep self-assurance is what attracts others to follow. They can trust their skills and don't need to establish themselves by force or by frightening others. They can also be coached to focus their ferocious energy toward bigger plans and projects, to fight more worthy battles.

Stage 2 Kings who are moving into Stage 3 will be more selective about projects they commit to, choosing those that require less force to accomplish. They will be more calmly self-confident themselves and will attract followers who are also more self-confident and self-respecting.

STAGE 3: These Kings can be highly effective. They are driven by a sense of purpose and, using their skills as master strategists, they eagerly tackle large-scale projects that result in entire system overhauls or paradigm shifts. Their projects no longer look like bloody skirmishes but more like well-orchestrated troop movements. Though still somewhat intimidating, Kings at this stage are very attractive to followers who are eager to contribute to the grand schemes these Kings present. A King in this stage has learned to be discerning in choosing followers for their aptitude and integrity and now delegates very well. But Kings still insist on unquestioning dedication and total alignment to their goals and plans from their team.

Stage 3 Kings can be encouraged to take on even grander projects and to consider that by giving up some level of control to their followers, their influence can grow exponentially. To expand their reach, these Kings must continue to focus on selecting only the best people and the most worthy projects. This King signals that they are moving to the next stage when their projects and plans entice top people to join them and they begin to give others a level of authority and include them in their planning.

STAGE 4: This fully developed King can now make a maximum contribution to their world and those around them. They have developed impressive precision in knowing just which projects to pursue and in having the very best people to make them happen. Rather than coercing or even persuading their followers regarding their plans, they elicit buy-in from them. This, in turn, makes for smooth and superior implementation. As they graciously share power with others, this noble King has the capacity to shift existing paradigms and influence existing systems with seeming ease. Though gentler and less overt in wielding their authority, this magnanimous leader is now powerful enough to revolutionize an entire industry, sphere of influence or area of interest on a grand scale.

KING SWEET SPOT—KEY POINTS

CORE VALUES & BEHAVIORS

- power, direction, purpose
- biggest picture, strategic planning
- paradigm shifting, destruction
- mastery, authority, decisiveness, delegation
- charisma, majesty, fearlessness, ambition
- integrity, strong internal compass

TRIGGERS

- incompetence
- disrespect of their authority
- control (of them)

CHALLENGES

- narcissism, grandiosity, arrogance, self-serving attitude and behavior
- authoritarianism, intolerance, ruthlessness, oppression, "turf building"
- stubbornness, refusal to cooperate, ignoring rules
- standoffishness, aloofness
- intimidation, unapproachability

GREAT ORGANIZATIONAL ROLES

- board of directors, senior advisor, leadership consultant
- executive, leader
- master strategist

THE KING LEADER

- sees from the highest perspective, implements new paradigms, directs very large projects
- wills things into existence
- follows own knowing, own compass
- surrounds themselves with extremely competent, masterful people
- sets direction, delegates, destroys

TIPS & COACHING:
LEVERAGING YOUR KING TALENT

If you discover you've got the King Sweet Spot while reading this chapter, these are ways you can experience the most joy, ease and collaboration and create the best results:

> Listen to your strong and loud **internal compass** and let it guide you—Kings have a powerful knowing that runs through the core of their body

- Learn to distinguish this **calm, grounded and solid** message (your internal knowing) and trust it
- When you have an opinion or perspective, notice if it comes from your internal compass or from concerns about possibly giving up power (these concerns will be sharper and quicker)

> Put your energy into **BIG projects** that you lead and steer— Kings naturally see from a 10,000-foot level

- You'll enjoy steering bigger projects with lots of moving parts; if this isn't easily available in your current position, you can likely create projects on the side
- Give yourself the time and opportunities to absorb whatever you need about systems, relationships, information, politics, etc., that allow you to see the **paradigms** at play and create new paradigms of your own
- Design strategies and leverage opportunities that set you up to play a bigger game over time; have every step build your power and promote yourself

> **Get intimate with anger**, both its healthy gifts and its dark shadows—Kings are able to tap rich creativity that is sourced from anger

- Explore the differences (e.g., by reading, working with respected teachers) between anger and aggression, so you take action in healthy ways
- Kings are the most comfortable with destruction, knowing it is essential to make space for what's next
- Listen to your anger—it isn't only needed for destruction (typically thoughts of "I don't want"); it is also important in creation (which is based in thoughts of "I want")
- Use your skills with **destruction** strategically; clear space for what's next confidently and calmly in ways that are less likely to scare off your followers and thereby sabotage your plans
- Reactive aggression might arise when you sense someone wanting to control you; instead, remind yourself of and reconnect to your **deep sense of power**; **take a stand** of "no" from a place of healthy anger—when you deeply know that

no one can control you, then no one can

> Let your confidence, demonstrated capability and **charisma** attract great people that you can **delegate** to—Kings need to design systems and delegate rather than be on the ground
  - Look for great people to be on your team and trust that as you're simply being who you are, great people will show up
  - Since Kings tend to be private, ensure you are public enough so that the great people can find you—your reputation will naturally precede you
  - If someone doesn't work out, be done with them (see the section on anger and destruction)

> **Treat your people well and empower them**—Kings are only as good as their plans are implemented
  - You'll get more from your followers when you treat them well, and if you truly know your own power, their growing power won't be threatening to you
  - Empowering and growing your followers will make you that much more enticing to others

> Choose **personal advisors** to grow yourself—Kings prefer to work privately and with experts
  - Identify the most competent people in their fields to learn from and develop one-on-one relationships
  - Honor your desire for privacy; however, don't let this hold you back from developing yourself
  - Sometimes Kings tend to avoid other Kings (over concerns about competing empires); however, when a senior King is respected, they could potentially be your best advisor

TIPS & COACHING: WORKING WITH A KING

If you discover you are managing or working with someone who has the King Sweet Spot:

> Honor their **power**—or it will only come back to bite you
>   • The King will be focused on promoting themselves, so you'll do best to empower them in ways that also empower you
>   • Listen to their strategies, consult them on paradigms and leveraging opportunities and never criticize or otherwise embarrass them or their ideas in front of others
>   • Be available as a mentor or resource in your areas of expertise, and they'll respect and appreciate you
>   • Kings are usually great at playing politics, so don't waste energy playing against them, as you'll likely lose—instead, collaborate or have them advise you on navigating politics
>   • Kings are often private, so don't expect them to show all their cards in front of others, such as in meetings—one-on-one conversations are often more productive

> Encourage them to follow their **internal compass**—this produces the best results
>   • Kings have a strong and loud internal compass that may seem uncooperative and domineering, but it is actually their greatest gift when used well
>   • Coach them to know and trust this calm and grounded inner power and to follow the pathways they see
>   • If needed, assist them with recognizing this internal compass and privately appreciate them for taking action

> Give them *BIG* **projects** to lead or advise on—they are natural leaders

- Encourage them to step up or reward them for already doing so
- Offer them leadership opportunities and people to delegate to
- Coach and support them to keep a big-picture perspective and to strategize
- Remind them that they are often able to powerfully and simply lead with their charisma

> Remind them that **collaboration** is essential—they are working on a team

- Refocus them on how collaborating with and respecting others will enable them to have more influence
- Encourage them to connect with others who are the most competent, to develop trust in them and to use them as resources
- Encourage the King to share how important integrity and follow-through are to them
- Recommend they explain their decisions, particularly choices of what to destroy, so others better understand
- You may need to empower others to share opinions that differ from the King's perspective; if needed, remind the King that they hate and don't trust "yes people," so they really want to hear these contradictory views

> Coach the King to understand how **aggression** and desire to have **power over others** actually gets in their way

- Give them feedback about when they are being decisive and clear (healthy anger) vs. when they are being aggressive and intimidating (anger's dark side)
- Remind them that if they attempt to grow their power by intimidating their followers, the strong ones will leave, and they will be left with a weaker team, thereby weakening themselves

FAMOUS KINGS

Alfred Hitchcock	John Muir	Plato
Alfred Lord Tennyson	John Rockefeller	Raisa Gorbachev
Aristotle Onassis	JP Morgan	Samuel Morse
Fidel Castro	Katherine Hepburn	Steven Harrison
Francisco Franco	King Louis XIV	Thomas Ridge
Gandhi	Mao Tse-tung	Tony Robbins
Golda Meir	Margaret Thatcher	William Taft
Jean Paul Getty	Pablo Picasso	

SYNTHESIZING YOUR REFLECTIONS

SUMMARIZING YOUR TALENTS

Now that you've read through all of the Talents, it's time to synthesize your reflections. We suggest you use the chart on the next page to help you organize your insights.

Remember, while you were reading about the Talents, you may have experienced the following:

- "Yes, that's me!" (exhilaration)
- "I wish I were or should be more like that." (envy)
- "No, that's not me." (neutrality or repulsion)

Or, as you put aside what you've been told all your life about who you are, what you should be or what you've been highly trained to do, you may have been able to try on and imagine behaving like each Talent. You might have discovered you felt:

- Energized or drained
- Alive or dull
- At ease or tense

	Yes, that's me! (exhilaration) **I HAVE THIS TALENT**	I wish I were or should be more like that. (envy) **THIS COULD BE MASKING**	No, that's not me. (neutrality or repulsion) **I DON'T HAVE THIS TALENT**
ARTISAN Creativity			
PRIEST Vision			
SAGE Communi-cation			
WARRIOR Efficiency			
SERVER Love			
SCHOLAR Know-ledge			
KING Power			

Now, take a step back to review the whole chart and see if this really feels like you.

Ideally, you have 3 Talents that stand out as yours. If you have more or fewer, that's okay. If you identify with five or more, consider that you may have the Artisan Talent (Artisans don't want to be boxed in and are the most adaptable).

If you are having trouble identifying your Talents, consider going back through the chapters to skim over the bolded words and review the stages of development, key points, and tips. Notice how you emotionally respond. Sit with this. See if this brings you more clarity. Remember, this is a journey. The discovery happens in layers, and the process itself is valuable for your growth.

Notice if one or both of your parents might have the Talents you marked in the second column as possible Masking and optionally note which parent, as this will likely stimulate insights.

PUTTING YOUR 3 TALENTS IN ORDER

As we've mentioned, each person has 3 Talents. It is the combination of these together that is your Sweet Spot. In addition to knowing what your 3 Talents are, it is also valuable to know their order of priority: 1st, 2nd and 3rd.

Your 1st Talent is the most important one; it is in the deepest core of your being. Your 2nd and 3rd Talents are also important; however, they're not as important as your 1st.

Your 1st Talent is at the heart of who you are; it is how you naturally **BE** in the world.

Your 2nd Talent is what you likely **DO** in life.

Your 3rd Talent is likely how you most easily **LEARN**.

Knowing the order of your 3 Talents will help you more quickly integrate them and access their power.

Your 3 Talents likely matured in a specific order and impacted particular aspects of your life. The table below may help you identify which are your 1st, 2nd and 3rd Talents. Typically, each Talent:

3rd	2nd	1st
develops in childhood	develops in teen, adolescent and young adult years	develops in adulthood
is how we most easily **LEARN**	is what we often **DO** in life	is at the heart of who we are, effortless, and how we **BE** in the world
was helpful in navigating our family of origin	was a major influence on our career choice	produces our best work
is what we do when tired and stressed, which also causes further exhaustion and anxiety	doing too much of this contributes to a "mid-life crisis" as we grow from our 2nd to our 1st	allows us to experience the most ease, joy and fulfillment

As the table above shows, we usually grow in reverse order, in that we typically grow into the most important one last. We typically express our 3rd Talent when young, then add our 2nd Talent and finally grow into our 1st Talent. Not everyone grows in this order, but this is common.

The figure below shows the journey of how we ideally grow from our Masks to *Learning* to *Doing* to *Being*. Also, with growth and maturation, the proportion of each Talent we express changes. As a healthy adult, we ideally express our 1st Talent most, supported by some of our 2nd Talent and even less of our 3rd. Most people are part way through this journey.

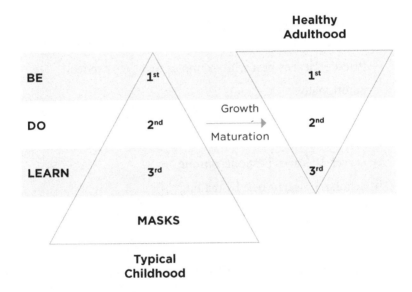

Answering these questions may help you clarify the order of your 3 Talents:

- Is there a Talent that is the easiest and most fulfilling for you? Is there a Talent that, to you, seems almost invisible because it is the "water you swim in?" **If so, this Talent may be your 1st.**

- Is there a Talent that you expressed a lot during your teen and early adult years? Is there a Talent that had a strong influence on your career choice? **If so, this Talent may be your 2nd.** (If Artisan is your 2nd, it may mean you've had a lot of different careers.)
- Is there a Talent that best describes how you like to learn? **If so, this Talent may be your 3rd.**

Each Talent typically learns in this way:

- Artisan 3rd learns in diverse ways (e.g., reading, listening, seeing visuals, doing hands-on activities, interacting one-on-one and joining a group)
- Priest 3rd learns best with examples that they can feel emotionally
- Sage 3rd learns most easily by joining a group
- Warrior 3rd learns best by doing
- Server 3rd learns best one-on-one
- Scholar 3rd learns best by reading
- King 3rd learns best in private or from a respected advisor

Keep in mind—if you are not able to narrow down to 3 Talents or put them in order, it's not a big deal. The impact of each Talent on different phases of your life may seem subtle and be hard to recognize. Exploring over time, getting feedback from others or possibly working with a coach typically provides more insight.

INTEGRATING YOUR 3 TALENTS INTO YOUR SWEET SPOT

Integrating your 3 Talents into your Sweet Spot looks really simple on paper; however, it is not often as simple in practice. We invite you to appreciate yourself for this life journey you have been on and to explore and play as you open to a new phase of your self-expression.

The growth journey of deepening into your Sweet Spot is a series of steps:

- identifying and loosening your Masks
- identifying your 3 Talents and putting them in order in your life
- shifting toward expressing your 1st Talent in the largest amount, followed by some of your 2nd Talent, and then even less of your 3rd Talent
- growing through the Stages of Development of your 3 Talents

These steps don't need to be done in order; they can be done simultaneously. Making progress in each of these areas opens up more joy, fulfillment, success and ease.

A DEEPER DIVE INTO THE SWEET SPOT

While the Talents are the "big rocks," the Sweet Spot also includes a wealth of other traits that can be explored. Altogether, your Sweet Spot encompasses:

- **Talents**—your natural skills and values
- **Pacing**—your natural rhythm or speed

- **Decision-Making**—your process for making choices
- **Communication**—how you integrate new awareness and express yourself
- **Motivation**—an underlying goal that impacts all you do
- **Defense**—how you automatically protect yourself
- **World View**—how you define success

Just as the Talents have 7 different options (Priest, Server, Sage, Artisan, King, Warrior and Scholar), each of these additional traits listed above has a range of options as well. In our work, we combine all of these traits together and call them the Sweet Spot because when a person knows, lives, works, and relates from this place, they thrive.

We offer Sweet Spot assessments and coaching, plus we are developing additional materials that explore these topics in depth and can be used to more fully understand and empower yourself, others, your interactions and your decisions.

CLIENT APPLICATIONS
OF THE SWEET SPOT

Throughout the book, we've provided many examples of how to use knowledge of your Sweet Spot for personal growth and leadership development. During the last decade, we've used the Sweet Spot in many different ways that have impacted organizations and leaders, professionally and personally.

By understanding themselves, leaders are able to use knowledge of their natural Talents and natural ways of interacting to feel more confident, trust their opinions and let go of unnatural expectations they've imposed on themselves. As a result, they build more credibility and respect from their teams and colleagues. We've seen so many clients experience more success, receive promotions, take on new initiatives and start new businesses—all things that did not seem likely to succeed or even be possible before knowing about their Sweet Spot.

The leaders we've worked with have also used knowledge of the Sweet Spot with their employees and colleagues to facilitate and empower their relationships. They know better how to honor the diversity of those around them, set people up for success, provide motivating feedback and build appreciation and trust that fuels collaboration.

By knowing the strengths of their colleagues, these leaders know whom best to seek out to brainstorm (Artisan), strategize (Warrior), align the team (Priest), soothe a colleague (Server), etc. They also know how to motivate people with different Talents by speaking to them about the things they value, using language that is the most meaningful. When messy situations happen, they now understand why and what to do about it.

The Sweet Spot provides powerful and immediate insight into team dynamics; often the first thing we do to understand a new client is a Sweet Spot Assessment of their leadership team. Based on their assessments, we are able to predict who is happy and fulfilled, who is frustrated with whom, what challenges and opportunities they have, which people likely work better together, and how to best navigate whatever situations they are facing.

Many clients have used the Sweet Spot in talent management and leadership development—growing and developing their people, including it in the decision-making process about whom to promote and hire, and facing when some employees are simply not a right fit. Some clients have moved employees to new positions where they've experienced great success, such as moving a VP of Operations to VP of Sales. And other times, we've used the Sweet Spot to help clients feel confident that the best decision is to let an employee go.

The best organizational roles for each Talent in Stages of Development 2-3 are shown in the following figure.

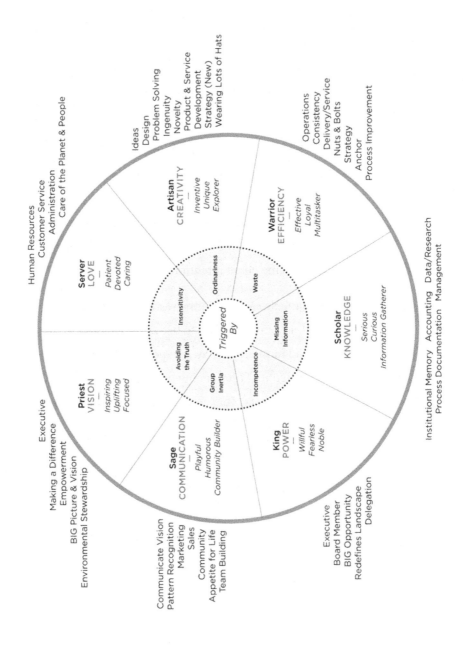

Businesses have also used the Sweet Spot to understand patterns in their culture and to make changes. For example, many entrepreneurial organizations have a lot of Artisans; they've often had lessons in recognizing and appreciating Warriors so they can scale their business. The Sweet Spot has also been useful for strategizing how to merge two cultures in acquisitions.

The Sweet Spot has been useful for clients to better understand their customers and design their marketing materials to more effectively reach them. Salespeople have used recognition of other people's Sweet Spots to customize how they speak about their products and services—converting more leads into sales, closing bigger deals and increasing client retention.

In addition to using the Sweet Spot in the workplace, many clients have brought it home—using it to better understand their romantic partners and families. The Sweet Spot is helpful in raising children to be authentic, experiencing more ease in the family and choosing fulfilling careers. The Sweet Spot has also been used very successfully for romantic matchmaking!

When you relax into your Sweet Spot, when you appreciate your journey and open to expanding more deeply into being who you really are, the applications are limitless.

ACKNOWLEDGMENTS

This book and our success wouldn't have been possible without the contributions of so many. We won't name them all, and we are compelled to highlight a few.

First, thank you to our clients and friends, many of whom actively gave feedback and support to us throughout the years while we focused our insights and put thought to paper. They have helped us shape a book that not only reflects their real-time experience and the power of knowing their Sweet Spot, it reflects their belief in us personally as well. We appreciate their support in championing us to the finish line!

Our colleagues have also been key to the fulfillment of this project. We want to mention Katie Lucas, our steadfast partner in the office (Scholar, Server and Artisan Talents) for all of her coordination and logistical support. And thank you to Don Myers, Eliza Prall, Mike Valentine, Heidi Ganahl, John Hagan, Alecia Huck, Lisa Banner, Arthur Brock, Tom Faggiano, Celeste Miracle, Sarah White Carr and the entire Culture Counts team.

Finally, we'd like to appreciate Larry Byram and his community. Larry was our first teacher in this work of identifying and appreciating our authentic expressions in ways that are similar to our Sweet Spot distinctions. Larry served as our teacher, coach and mentor. He encouraged us to partner with each other, even when we thought the idea was crazy, because he saw what we could contribute to each other in the building of our work. He was right! And we sincerely thank him for bringing his gift to the world so we could learn and, from that foundation, develop our own flavor of this work and soar.

ABOUT THE AUTHORS

WHITNEY WALPOLE has been a trusted partner and professional leadership coach to hundreds of business owners and executive teams over the past 18 years. After teaching in public schools early in her career, Whitney cofounded a private school and later a software development company. She later founded Culture Counts, a firm offering coaching and consulting to leaders who want to increase their effectiveness and self-awareness. Whitney is also an inspiring speaker who engages her audiences to step into leadership and create successful organizations they love. Whitney is passionate about growth, and when she isn't working with others, she is spending her time with her family, cats, traveling and expanding her own ability to lead and love. Whitney's Sweet Spot includes Priest, Artisan and Scholar Talents. Learn more about Whitney and her work at www.culturecounts.biz.

LAURELI SHIMAYO has been a coach and consultant specializing in applying Sweet Spot and body psychology to leadership development, human resources and romantic matchmaking for 8 years. After applying her training in molecular biology to medicine, agriculture and intellectual property, helping launch a consumer-product startup and working with Culture Counts since 2009, she now runs her own coaching and consulting firm. Laureli brings a brilliantly insightful and intuitive mind together with an engaging and present heart. She is at her core a "connectress"—connecting knowledge into a useful map, organizations with ways to win their game, people with their purpose and genius, complementary teammates and partners to each other and people into deeper connection. Laureli's Sweet Spot includes Scholar, Warrior and Sage Talents. Learn more about Laureli and her work at www.LaureliShimayo.com and more about all the Sweet Spot traits including the 7 Talents at www.ThriveTypes.com.

HOW TO REACH US

Contact Whitney Walpole and Culture Counts at:

303-872-7926

Info@culturecounts.biz

www.culturecounts.biz

Contact Laureli Shimayo and learn more about the Sweet Spot at:

720-352-2434

Laureli@ThriveTypes.com

www.ThriveTypes.com

Culture Counts is a coaching and consulting firm specializing in helping business leaders create better business results by shaping great workplace cultures.

Our services include leadership coaching, training and development, culture strategy and assessment, and workshops and retreats. We are also available for speaking engagements.

If you would like to further explore your Sweet Spot, we also do in-depth assessments for individuals and teams. These assessments identify and clarify all your Sweet Spot distinctions:

- **Talents**—your natural skills and values
- **Pacing**—your natural rhythm or speed
- **Decision-Making**—your process for making choices
- **Communication**—how you integrate new awareness and express yourself
- **Motivation**—an underlying goal that impacts all you do
- **Defense**—how you automatically protect yourself
- **World View**—how you define success

One of our specialties is helping people see through their Masking to identify their true Sweet Spot. Many personality assessment tools used in the workplace are not able to do this well. We look forward to supporting you and your team to see through your Masks to your Sweet Spots so you thrive.

The authors' Sweet Spot distinctions include:

WHITNEY: Priest, Artisan and Scholar Talents, Growth Motivation, Think Feel Act to Fluid Communication, Switchable to Variable Decision-Making, Structured to Fluid Defense, Quick to Variable Pacing, and Fulfillment to Presence World View

LAURELI: Scholar, Warrior and Sage Talents, Growth Motivation, Think Feel Act to Fluid Communication, Variable Decision-Making, Switchable to Fluid Defense, Variable Pacing, and Fulfillment to Presence World View

Made in the USA
Monee, IL
11 February 2020

21614330R00128